# God's Little Devotional Book

## for African Americans

HONOR **HB** BOOKS

*Inspiration and Motivation for the Seasons of Life*

COOK COMMUNICATIONS MINISTRIES
Colorado Springs, Colorado • Paris, Ontario
KINGSWAY COMMUNICATIONS LTD
Eastbourne, England

*The Lord does not measure out our afflictions according to our faults,
but according to our strength,
and looks not at what we have deserved,
but what we are able to bear.*

George Downame

# Introduction

God has a plan for your life that is specific to you and no one else. Like everyone, however, you are faced with challenges and obstacles every day that have been designed by the devil to keep you from focusing on God and seeking His will for your life.

That is why *God's Little Devotional Book for African Americans* was written. It is filled with heartfelt devotions and reflections about people just like you—people who faced the same challenges, same obstacles, and same distractions as you—on their way to walking in victory and becoming successful. Their powerful stories and the life principles they applied will inspire you to see a God who knows where you live, what you face, and how to bring you to the Source of strength, healing, and renewed faith.

As you read through the pages of this inspiring book about real-life people, you will be motivated and encouraged to "take a quiet break" from the busyness of the day and discover how much God loves you and intends to see that you become all He created you to be. Not only will you be inspired to build a closer personal relationship with Him and to have a stronger confidence in yourself, you will also be given the tools to establish life-transforming habits and attitudes.

It is our prayer that this book will draw you into a life that exhibits the heart of God and rekindle your faith and love for Him.

*Success is to be measured not so much
by the position that one has reached in life
as by the obstacles which one has overcome
while trying to succeed.*

Growing up in a poor Black section of Detroit, Ben became used to the title "the dumbest kid in the fifth grade." After all, he had the grades—mostly zeros—to prove it. And if ever he lost sight of that fact, the entire fifth grade class stood ready to remind him.

Despite a midterm report that confirmed their opinion, Ben knew he was not as dumb as his classmates claimed.

Ben's mother finally told him and his brother, Curtis, that she would pray and ask God to show her how to help her sons improve their grades.

"If you keep making grades like this, you'll spend the rest of your life sweeping floors in a factory," Ben's mother told them. "And that's not what God wants for you!"

Two days later, the boys learned how God intended to answer their mother's prayer.

"You may choose two TV shows to watch each

week," she said. "We'll spend the rest of the time reading."

Though reluctant to follow that plan at first, the boys obeyed.

Ben adopted a regimen that included hours of reading at the local library. Soon, reading turned into learning. And over the years, learning became knowledge. Before long, the "dumbest kid in the fifth grade" found himself faced with the difficult decision of which college to attend—Harvard or Yale.

Today, Dr. Ben Carson is widely recognized as one of the nation's top neurosurgeons and most sought-after speakers.

What people think of you today does not determine what they will know of you tomorrow. God had a purpose for creating you, and He has a plan to see you succeed. Ask Him to help you see how He is working in your life. Then allow Him to guide you to becoming the success He intends for you to be.

*Do your best to present yourself to God*
*as one approved, a workman who does not*
*need to be ashamed and who correctly*
*handles the word of truth.*
2 TIMOTHY 2:15

Not all advice is good, but sometimes paying attention to the ideas of others can pay big dividends. Wally Amos learned that valuable lesson even as an already successful manager of some of the entertainment industry's biggest names.

Well established as an intelligent businessman, the charismatic, self-styled Amos left his job with a talent agency to manage his own clients. Having a flair for cooking, Amos often baked cookies and passed them out to people while attending meetings or visiting on the set at television and motion picture studios. The cookies were sometimes a bigger hit than Amos himself.

> The talent of success is nothing more than doing what you can do well, and doing well whatever you do, without a thought of fame.

"It reached the point that people wouldn't say 'Hello' when they saw me; they'd ask, 'Hey, where are my cookies?'" Amos would later recall. Before long, those same people were advising him to go into the cookie business.

It was good advice.

In March 1975, Amos borrowed $25,000 and

opened his first freestanding gourmet cookie store on Hollywood's Sunset Boulevard. Within months, he had two more stores and was selling his homespun chocolate chip cookies to many of the same people he had managed. Reporting on his newfound success, the media dubbed the "Famous Amos" product "the cookie of the jet set."

By 1980, Famous Amos cookies had grossed $5 million. Five years later, sales had doubled. Wally Amos, who went from managing people to managing cookies, was now a millionaire.

"I opened the first gourmet chocolate chip cookie store in the world and set off a culinary explosion," Amos would later explain. "All I wanted to do was make a living. I didn't even care about being famous."

It doesn't always take doing something big to become someone famous. Fame is sometimes achieved simply by doing what comes naturally. God knows how to use the little things—and people—to do great and mighty works. It's when you are faithful in what you have that He will give you more.

*Do not despise these small beginnings, for the LORD rejoices to see the work begin.*
ZECHARIAH 4:10 NLT

11

GLDB

> I pray the Good Lord to give us courage to recognize
> our weaknesses and wisdom to recognize the truth
> and, having recognized that truth, moral power to
> stay committed to it through thick and thin.

Prince Edward County in Virginia found its way into the history books in the late 1950s when authorities decided to close their public schools rather than desegregate them. During that five-year period from 1959 to 1964—a time later referred to as "the crippled generation"—many of the county's 1,700 Black students went without any formal education.

But attention had been brought to the county's racial ills years before in 1951, when a sixteen-year-old student named Barbara Johns led a strike to protest poor conditions at her all-Black high school. A bright, articulate sixteen-year-old whose only desire was a shot at the American dream, Barbara had become frustrated when the local school board showed little concern for the adverse conditions at the all-Black Robert Russa Moton High School in Farmville, Virginia. Close to 450 students attended the school—more than twice the 180 students it was built to accommodate.

Rather than build a new school, the board erected tar-paper shacks outside the school to handle the overflow. Classes were also held in school buses and in the school's auditorium.

Upset at the school board's lack of concern, Johns met in secret with several students and organized a strike. Within weeks, the local NAACP had sued the county, asking that all schools be integrated. The Farmville case became one of the five cases that the U.S. Supreme Court reviewed in *Brown v. Board of Education of Topeka* when it declared segregation unconstitutional in 1954. In 1964, a Supreme Court ruling forced local authorities to fund public education and reopen the schools.

There may be times when standing up for what you know is right may seem pointless, but it is always the right thing to do. You're not fighting alone. God is always on your side, and He will give you the strength and courage you need to stand. Just ask Him.

*Be strong and courageous. Do not be afraid or terrified because of them, for the LORD your God goes with you; he will never leave you nor forsake you.*
DEUTERONOMY 31:6

In the song "Nature Boy," popular singer Nat "King" Cole delivers a heartfelt message in lyrics that state: "The greatest thing you'll ever learn is just to love and be loved in return."

Love may have been a priority with Cole, who conquered the pop charts and won thousands of enduring fans during the fifties and sixties with the success of such well-orchestrated ballads as "Mona Lisa," "Unforgettable," and "Ramblin' Rose"; but on a number of occasions during his career, the smooth-voiced singer found that not everyone shared his feelings about peace and harmony. As did most Black entertainers of his era, Cole endured his share of hatred and bigotry.

> Love conquers all things; let us give in to love.

When Cole and his wife bought a house in the exclusive Hancock Park section of Los Angeles in 1949, for example, neighbors formed an association to prevent them from moving in. In the mid-fifties, at the height of his career, the famed singer was even attacked by a group of white men while performing in Birmingham, Alabama.

Presented to:

_LeLani F. London_

From:

_Mom - Sylvia Flores_
Love you -

Date:

_5 / 10 / 2007_

# God's Little Devotional Book

## for African Americans

Honor Books® is an imprint of
Cook Communications Ministries, Colorado Springs, Colorado 80918
Cook Communications, Paris, Ontario
Kingsway Communications, Eastbourne, England

God's Little Devotional Book for African Americans
© 2005 by Honor Books

Printed in Canada
First printing, 2005

3 4 5 6 7 8 9 10 Printing/Year  10 09 08 07 06

Developed by Bordon Books
Manuscript written by Ronald C. Jordan
Editorial by SnapdragonGroup Editorial Services
Designed by Koechel Peterson and Associates

ISBN-13: 978-1-5629-2216-0
ISBN-10: 1-5629-2216-5

people that it was far from proper for them to bear the surname of their former owners, and a great many of them took other surnames. This was one of the first signs of freedom. When they were slaves, a coloured person was simply called "John" or "Susan." There was seldom occasion for more than the use of the one name. If "John" or "Susan" belonged to a white man by the name of "Hatcher," sometimes he was called "John Hatcher," or as often "Hatcher's John." But there was a feeling that "John Hatcher" or "Hatcher's John" was not the proper title by which to denote a freeman; and so in many cases "John Hatcher" was changed to "John S. Lincoln" or "John S. Sherman," the initial "S" standing for no name, it being simply a part of what the coloured man proudly called his "entitles."

Knowing who you are and for what purpose you were created by God enables you to know where you are going.

*It is for freedom that Christ has set us free.*
*Stand firm, then, and do not let yourselves*
*be burdened again by a yoke of slavery.*
GALATIANS 5:1

In the biography, *Having Our Way: The Delany Sisters' First 100 Years*, Sarah "Sadie" Delany, then 104 years old, recalled what strict disciplinarians her parents were and how much influence they had on their ten children.

"Papa was the head of the house, though he always made sure we treated Mama with great respect," Sadie Delany said in the book she coauthored with her 102-year-old sister, Bessie, in 1993.

"Each morning, Papa would make us line up for our 'inspection.' He'd look us over to see if our shoes were polished, our ears were clean, things like that. He was proud of his children, and I think this was just a way for him to convey this. We carried the Delany name, and he wanted us to look respectable when we left the house."

> I'm very pleased with each advancing year. It stems back to when I was forty. I was a bit upset about reaching that milestone, but an older friend consoled me. "Don't complain about growing old—many people do not have that privilege."

Following their parents' lead, Sadie and sister Bessie put strong emphasis on education—an effort that eventually established them as pioneering African-American professionals.

The daughters of a man born into slavery who became America's first elected Black Episcopal bishop, the two sisters began their education at Saint Augustine's College in Raleigh, North Carolina.

Bessie graduated from Columbia University, where she received a Doctor of Dental Surgery degree. In 1923, she became the first Black woman licensed in New York to practice dentistry. Sadie earned bachelor's and master's degrees from Columbia University's Teacher's College and was the first Black teacher in the New York school system to teach domestic science on the high school level.

Neither sister ever married. Both died in the 1990s—Bessie in 1995 at age 104 and Sadie in 1999 at age 109. Their accomplishments, during a time when Black women in America were given little opportunity to succeed, stand as memorials forever etched in the history of this nation.

With God in the picture, "little opportunity to succeed" becomes "every opportunity to succeed." Do your best with what He's given you, and trust Him with your future. Soon you will find that He will cause doors once tightly locked to spring open before you.

*"I will satisfy them with a long life*
*and give them my salvation."*

PSALM 91:16 NLT

GLDB

> On becoming more acquainted with the words
> of the Bible, I began to understand so much more
> of what I had been taught, and of what I had
> learned about life and about the people in mine.

"It did seem to me sometimes that Reverend Jasper came into the world with a Bible in his heart, head, and tongue."

That's how an anonymous minister once described John Jasper, a former slave. After coming to know Christ as his Savior in 1839, he used an old spelling book to teach himself to read, then embarked on an exhaustive study of the Bible—committing much of Scripture to memory.

It seems that the Reverend Jasper knew the importance of God's Word in his everyday life. So much so that not only did he take the time to commit it to memory, but he hid it in his heart. Consequently, after becoming a minister of the Gospel, Jasper preached before hundreds of congregations—including delivering a stirring message before members of the Virginia General Assembly. As history records, Jasper's sermons were powerfully effective in the lives of many who gave themselves to the Lord after hearing this fiery Black preacher speak.

God considers you one of His ambassadors on the earth to carry the message of His Word to the people. If you are diligent to study God's Word and hold it in your heart as well as in your head, you, too, can be effective in leading men and women out of darkness and into the light. When you know firsthand what it's like to be delivered from bondage, you can share an encouraging word that will not only set others free, but give them a life of everlasting hope.

*I have hidden your word in my heart.*
PSALM 119:11

The e-mail requesting help for a young amputee who needed a prosthesis was all too familiar for Craig. Just a few years earlier, the former police officer had himself lost a leg after being attacked in the line of duty.

The first night after the incident, Craig's thoughts were running rampant as he lay awake in a hospital bed. Questions raced through his mind: How would he care for is family? Would he ever be able to play ball with his son?

He posed those same questions to God.

Craig's pessimistic attitude was countered by his wife's optimism. She confidently encouraged her husband with an assurance that some wa somehow, they would tun their tragedy into triumph.

*If you and I don't build a bridge back, throw out some strong lifelines to our children, youth, and families whom poverty and unemployment are engulfing, they're going to drown, pull many of us down with them and undermine the future our forebearers dreamed, struggled, and died for.*

The turn began one nigl t when, while still in the hospital and preparing to be fitted with a prosthesis, Craig saw a young patient who had also lost a leg—to cancer. The boy's family, Craig was told, could not afford the cost of an artificial limb.

A few days later, Craig prayed and asked God to show him what he could do to help the boy. The answer came quickly. Craig and his wife decided to pass on part of the money raised for Craig's artificial leg. Compassion did not stop there. The following year, Craig and a friend started a foundation to provide financial support for needy amputees—an organization that so far has provided help for more than six thousand people.

When tragedy strikes, many people strike out at God demanding to know, "Why me?" This question only invites anger and resentment. A sincere concern for the afflictions endured by others, on the other hand, can stimulate healing and hope.

*Live in harmony with one another; be sympathetic, love as brothers, be compassionate and humble.*
1 PETER 3:8

GLDB

> *Who ran to help me when I fell,*
>
> *or kissed the place to make it well?*
>
> *My mother.*

In a hurry to cool off on a hot summer day in south Florida, a young boy was unaware that an alligator occupied the same water hole he was about to dive into. Seconds later, the reptile began a slow but intense movement toward the youngster.

From a window inside their home, the boy's mother caught a glimpse of her son swimming—and the approach of the alligator. Dashing from the house and running toward the water, the mother yelled for her son to swim to shore.

By the time the boy turned around and finally reached shore, it was too late. His mother desperately tried to pull him from the water by his arms, but the alligator held a firm grip on his legs. A tug-of-war ensued, pitting a compassionate mother against an aggressive alligator. It continued until a farmer who was passing by heard the screams, grabbed his shotgun, and killed the alligator.

After weeks in the hospital, the boy was released to go home. His legs were severely scarred from the alligator's attack, and his arms bore deep scratches where his mother's fingernails had dug deep into his flesh as she held on to him for dear life.

When the media interviewed the boy some weeks later, a reporter asked to see his scars. Lifting his pant legs, the boy showed off the teeth marks left by the alligator. Then, with obvious pride, he showed the reporter his arms.

"I have great scars on my arms too," he told the reporter. "I have them because my mom wouldn't let go."

It's never good to dwell on the past. But sometimes it's not a bad idea to look at the scars of your past— unsightly reminders of sin that kept you in bondage— in a new way. They also serve to remind you of the loving Savior who came and rescued you and pulled you out of a pit. When sin was pulling on you so hard, God never let go.

*Rescue me from the mouth of the lions;*
*save me from the horns of the wild oxen.*
PSALM 22:21

Growing up in a segregated Birmingham, Alabama, Condoleezza Rice may have had every reason to believe she would never amount to anything. But John and Angelena Rice prepared Condoleezza and her siblings for the future with well-rounded educations.

"Our parents really did have us convinced that even though I couldn't have a hamburger at Woolworth's, I could be president of the United States," Rice once told an interviewer.

These amazing parents also tried to protect their children from the horrors of racism in Birmingham. But Rice would eventually be affected by the violence and hatred that ravaged the racially tense city during the 1960s. Among the victims of the 1963 bombing of a Black church in the city was one of her kindergarten classmates.

*Most of the people who have scaled the heights, who have climbed the mountains, who have gone through the valleys of their lives have not been people who were contented to just stand.*

Rice encountered subtle racism, like the high school guidance counselor who said she was not college material—despite the fact that Rice was a straight-A student who excelled in Latin and was an accomplished figure skater and pianist.

Undaunted by such actions, Rice pressed her way up the ladder to a successful political career. After spending more than two decades as a professor of political science, her expert knowledge of the political machinations of the former Soviet Bloc made her a highly sought-after consultant in both the pubic and private sectors.

In January 2001, at age forty-seven, Rice became the first woman ever to be named National Security Advisor to the president of the United States. She later went on to become the president's Secretary of State in 2005.

Don't just accept what others say about you. God has given you the keys to your own destiny.

*Diligent hands will rule.*
PROVERBS 12:24

GLDB

> Your relationships with people begin in the home, where you learn values. It's the responsibility of the family.

As a youngster growing up in Mount Vernon, New York, Denzel Washington received solid family values from his parents, Lennis and Denzel Washington. Despite the fact that his parents divorced when he was only fourteen, an event that devastated Washington, he has always held on to what they taught him.

In his biography, the prolific actor said: "I always try to have my family with me when I am out in public," indicating the importance of removing the negative stereotype of the "one-parent" Black family and demonstrating that Black families can be cohesive.

In the area of his work as one of America's leading male actors, Washington has had another inspiration: "It was instilled in me as a young performer to take chances ... because failure is part of growth."

Washington took a chance when he decided to leave acting school after completing just the first year of a three-year program to pursue a fulltime acting career. At first there were failures, but perseverance and the support of a loving wife, like that of his parents, strongly encouraged Washington that he could make it. It was all Washington needed to keep pushing.

That "you can make it" attitude has stuck with Washington and brought him the success he enjoys today. An Academy Award winner with more than two dozen films to his credit, Washington is prominently recognized as one of America's ten favorite and most-respected actors.

Taking chances is a big part of life. But you never have to go it alone. God says He will always be with you, to ensure you make it through. When your strength is failing, remember God is right there with you. He will never leave you hanging out on a limb. So feel free to draw from His strength.

*Train a child in the way he should go, and when he is old he will not turn from it.*
PROVERBS 22:6

What are you planting in your spiritual garden? Here's how you can have a bumper crop.

Plant three rows of Ps:
1.   peace of mind
2.   peace of heart
3.   peace of soul

Plant four rows of squash:
1.   Squash gossip.
2.   Squash indifference.
3.   Squash grumbling.
4.   Squash selfishness.

Plant four rows of lettuce:
1.   Lettuce be faithful.
2.   Lettuce be kind.
3.   Lettuce be patient.
4.   Lettuce really love one another.

Plant three rows of turnips:
1.   Turnip for meetings.

> *You don't invent a tree; you plant it. You don't extract the fruit; you let it grow. A nation isn't a sudden creation, it's a slow ripening, year after year, ring after ring.*

2. Turnip for service.
3. Turnip to help one another.

Include three rows of thyme:
1. thyme for each other
2. thyme for family
3. thyme for friends

God desires for you to plant good seed so that you reap a bountiful crop of His blessings. He will give you more than enough to share with others.

*The fruit of the Spirit is love, joy, peace, patience, kindness, goodness, faithfulness, gentleness, self-control.*
GALATIANS 5:22-23 NASB

GLDB

> You're not more than anyone else
> and you're not less than, but you're
> just as much as anyone else.

The speaker began his seminar by holding up a twenty-dollar bill, and in a room filled with two hundred people, he asked the question: "Who would like this twenty-dollar bill?" Hands started going up. "I am going to give this to one of you, but first—" He then crumpled the bill. "Who wants it now?" Still the hands went up in the air.

"Well," he responded, "what if I do this?" The man dropped the bill to the floor, stomped on it, and began grinding it into the carpet with his shoe. Picking up the dirty, crumpled bill, he then asked again, "Now, who wants it?" Hands shot into the air.

Finally, the man said: "My friends, no matter what I did to the money, you still wanted it, because it did not decrease in value. It is still worth twenty dollars."

The same is true in the life of Jesus, who suffered great abuse and mistreatment. Even death on the cross could not diminish His value and the importance of

His mission in the world.

In a sense, life really is like a bed of roses. Although both are sprinkled with thorns, they do not lose their great value. In the course of your life, you may be mistreated, abused, and stepped on. But you never lose your value. Your worth comes not from what you have done or what others have done to you. You are valuable because you are God's unique creation and His beloved child.

*I praise you because I am fearfully*
*and wonderfully made; your works are wonderful,*
*I know that full well.*
PSALM 139:14

Curious as to its content, the son opened the box and found a lovely, leather-bound Bible with his name embossed in gold. Obviously disappointed, the son turned to his father and said, "With all your money, all you give me is a Bible?" Then the boy stormed out of the house, leaving the Bible behind.

Years passed, and the young man became a successful businessman with a beautiful home and a wonderful family. But in all those years, the son had not once seen his father. Now it seemed like the time was right to make amends. Before he could do so, however, the son received a telegram saying his father had died and had left him all his possessions.

*Gratitude is a nice touch of beauty added last of all to the countenance, giving a classic beauty, an angelic loveliness, to the character.*

Arriving at his father's house, the son began the task of looking through the papers on his father's desk. Just then, he saw the Bible his father had given him. Opening it, he turned the pages until he got to the book of Matthew, where a passage had been carefully underlined. It read: "If you, then, though you are evil, know how to give good gifts to your children, how much more will your Father in heaven give good gifts to those who ask him!" (Matthew 7:11).

As he read those words, a car key dropped from the back of the Bible. It bore a tag with a dealer's name on it—the same dealer who had had the sports car he had wanted so many years before.

On the tag was the date of his graduation and the words, "Paid in full."

Are you missing out on some of God's richest gifts because they didn't come wrapped the way you expected?

*I have learned to be content whatever the circumstances.*
PHILIPPIANS 4:11

> We have hard work to do,
> and loads to lift; shun not the
> struggle—face it; 'tis God's gift.

It was around 4:30 in the afternoon when four young African-American students from the Agricultural and Technical College in Greensboro, North Carolina, sat down at the lunch counter of a Woolworth's department store and asked to be served. They had chosen to ignore the stand-up bar at the end of the counter—the only section where Blacks were allowed to eat at the time.

Joseph McNeil, Ezell Blair Jr., Franklin McCain, and David Richmond were not expecting to be served when they entered the store, and they were not. Rather, the four were there to make a statement—that Blacks should be afforded the same courtesies as white people, especially when it came to pubic facilities.

Their action resulted in a standoff of sorts, with the four Black men demanding service and the waitresses refusing. When they left the store at the end of the day, a lone photographer from the local newspaper was waiting to take their pictures. Little did anyone know the impact that single incident would have on Greensboro, the state of North Carolina, or the nation.

Thirty years later, the same four men returned to the Woolworth's store in Greensboro, sat down at the same lunch counter, and asked to be served breakfast. They were served by the same two waitresses who, thirty years earlier, had refused to wait on them.

No lone reporter waited outside. Instead, media was gathered en masse to record this moment in history. The single sit-in these four had staged in 1960, as innocent, young college students, had ignited the Civil Rights Movement—a force that swept the nation and eventually resulted in the legislation that put an end to desegregation in the United States.

Ordinary people can do extraordinary things. God gives them that power—He gives that same power to you!

*Use every piece of God's armor to resist the enemy*
*in the time of evil, so that after the battle*
*you will still be standing firm.*
EPHESIANS 6:13 NLT

A successful young executive watched carefully as he drove his new Jaguar through the neighborhood, making sure that no child would dart out in front of his car. Suddenly, a brick smashed into the passenger-side door.

Slamming on the brakes, the man backed up to where the car had been hit. A young kid stood there waiting. He didn't move even as the executive jumped from the car and grabbed him by the arm.

"That's a new car, and that brick you threw is going to cost a lot of money," he screamed at the frightened youngster.

*As selfishness and complaint pervert and cloud the mind, so love with its joy clears and sharpens the vision.*

"Please, mister, please," the boy cried. "I didn't know what else to do. I threw the brick because no one else would stop."

With tears rolling down his face, the boy pointed to the other side of a parked car nearby.

"It's my brother. He rolled off the curb and fell out of his wheelchair. I've tried, but I can't lift him. Won't you please help me?"

Moved beyond words, the man lifted the young boy back into the wheelchair, then took out his handkerchief and wiped the boy's scrapes and cuts.

"Thank you and God bless you," the grateful child said to him.

The man watched as the little boy pushed his brother down the sidewalk toward their home. Then he began to walk back to his precious Jaguar.

He never did have the dent repaired. It was his reminder: never go through life so fast that someone has to throw a brick at you to get your attention.

God whispers to your soul and speaks to your heart. Sometimes when you don't have time to listen, He has to throw a "brick" at you. It's your choice: won't you listen to the whisper instead of waiting for the brick?

*"I called, but no one answered;*
*I spoke, but they did not listen."*
ISAIAH 66:4 NASB

> *There are seasons when new depths seem to be broken up in the soul, when new wants are unfolded and a new and undefined good is thirsted for. These are periods when to dare is the highest wisdom.*

With Chicago trailing by three points in the final minute, there was no question as to where the ball would end up. When it came down to the wire in a Chicago Bulls game, Michael Jordan was the designated go-to guy.

It was no different with the NBA final game in 1998. With 5.2 seconds left, Jordan sank the game-winning shot—a twenty-footer —that gave the Bulls an 87-86 victory over the Utah Jazz and their sixth NBA championship in eight years.

Jordan had overcome fatigue and finished the night with 45 points. That single shot would go down in history as the most memorable basketball moment of the 1990s. But as he recalls in his book, *Rare Air*, success for Jordan did not start with his risk-taking big shots in the NBA. It began several years earlier when, as a college freshman at the University of North Carolina, Jordan led his team to a National Collegiate Athletic

Association Division 1 championship.

"I wasn't afraid to take big shots in the professional ranks because I had made one when I was a snotty-nosed kid in 1982 to beat Georgetown," Jordan writes in the book. "I was fearless after that. Now when I get in that situation, I don't weigh the negatives and positives and hope the positives win. I just go back to my past successes, step forward, and respond. That's why your greatest players make great plays in clutch situations consistently."

When he officially retired from the sport after a brief stint with the Washington Wizards, Jordan had amassed an amazing record, undoubtedly garnering him the title of the greatest basketball player ever in America.

When it's difficult to trust God, consider all the times He has kept His promises in your life, helped you through difficult situations, given you the winning basket. Then go for it—your hesitation will quickly disappear.

*I remember the days of old. I ponder all your great works. I think about what you have done.*
PSALM 143:5 NLT

Feeling like he was at the end of his rope, the young man dropped to his knees and prayed: "Lord, I can't go on. My cross is too heavy to bear."

In a moment, he heard the voice of the Lord, saying: *If you can't bear the weight of your cross, my son, place it here. Then open this door and pick out any cross you wish.*

Filled with relief, the man said, "Thank You, Lord," and did as he had been told.

Upon opening the door, he saw many crosses. Some were so large the tops were not visible. Then, he spotted a tiny cross leaning against a far wall.

"I'd like that one, Lord," he whispered.

> People have to learn sometimes not only how much the heart, but how much the head, can bear.

In the quiet of that room, the man heard the Lord reply: *My son, that is the cross you just brought in.*

How easy it is to look at others and think everything is rosy and bright, but our circumstances seem so dark and gloomy. The grass may look greener on the other side of the fence, but at some point it still has to be mowed.

The Bible challenges us not to think we are the only ones who face certain tests and trials. They come to others as well. There is encouragement, however, in the fact that God is always present to help us through them. If we let Him, He will show us the way out.

When life's problems seem to be overwhelming, it may help to look around and see what other people are coping with. You may consider yourself far more fortunate than you imagined.

*No test or temptation that comes your way is beyond the course of what others have had to face. All you need to remember is that God will never let you down; he'll never let you be pushed past your limit; he'll always be there to help you come through it.*

1 CORINTHIANS 10:13 MSG

GLDB

> The past is a rich resource on which we can draw in order to make decisions for the future, but it does not dictate our choices. We should look back at the past and select what is good, and leave behind what is bad.

At first, the woman had been surrounded by compassionate, caring friends after the sudden loss of her husband, who died in a tragic accident. They brought meals, sent cards, telephoned, and prayed. But then the weeks turned into months, and it seemed like everyone had forgotten.

Now, no one was there to comfort her. She was alone except for the two small children she had been left to raise.

She longed to hear her husband's name mentioned in conversation. She yearned to talk about the wide stride of his walk, the warmth of his easy laugh, and how his hand had felt so strong around hers. She wanted the neighbors to come and borrow his tools or have a grown man play basketball with her sons.

But none of it ever happened.

Then came the first anniversary of her husband's death. The dew of the early morning was still wet on the grass as she walked across the cemetery lawn. That's when she saw it—lying next to her husband's gravestone. Someone had been there ahead of her and left behind a small bouquet of fresh-cut flowers, tied with a ribbon. It was a gentle, caring act that reached out to her lonely heart like a tender hug. With tears streaming down her cheeks, the woman read the unsigned note that accompanied the flowers. The words said simply, "I remember too."

When you feel abandoned and memories of the past are all you have to hold on to, remember that God is there to comfort you. Others may become preoccupied to the point of not calling, writing, or dropping by for a visit, but God never forgets about you. He's always there for you. Try talking with Him now.

*The LORD comforts his people and will have compassion on his afflicted ones. ...*
*"Can a mother forget the baby at her breast and have no compassion on the child she has borne? Though she may forget, I will not forget you!" ...*
*declares the LORD.*
ISAIAH 49:13,15,18

It is expected that teachers will encourage their students. But a young Morrie Turner was anything but encouraged to hear his grade-school teacher suggest he would never be successful—because he was Black.

"Too bad he's colored," Turner recalls hearing the Oakland grammar school teacher say. "That kid has talent, but he'll never make it in the art world."

Fortunately, the world was not as fixed on race as Turner's teacher was back then. And hopefully, the educator was around a few years later to see the impact "that kid" made on the art world.

A novice with no formal art training, Turner had been dabbling in cartooning since the fifth grade. Following a stint in the military—where he drew a series of comics for the *Stars and Stripes* called "Rail Head"—Turner began freelancing his work.

> Be careful, think about the effect of what you say. Your words should be constructive, bring people together, not pull them apart.

His first moneymaker paid five dollars. But his second, a cartoon he drew for an automobile-club

46

magazine, was accidentally sent to *Better Homes & Gardens* and brought him seventy-five dollars. As it turned out, the magazine was planning an article for women on how to repair their own cars—exactly what was depicted in Turner's cartoon.

When Turner asked cartoonist Charles Schultz why there were no minorities in cartoons, the creator of the famed *Peanuts* comic strip suggested Turner create one. By 1965, Turner's series *Dinky Fellas* had evolved into a strip called *Wee Pals*, the first multiethnic cartoon syndicated in the United States.

Today the cartoon, which not only opened doors for Turner but also paved the way for other African-American cartoonists, appears in more than one hundred newspapers across the country.

When others criticize you and call you a failure, remember what God says about you. Jesus called himself a vine, and you are a branch that springs from Him. He provides all the nutrients you need to flourish and produce good fruit, so draw on Him today.

*The right word at the right time is like*
*precious gold set in silver.*
PROVERBS 25:11 CEV

## Fear cannot live with faith.

In the aftermath of the 1954 Supreme Court ruling that called for the desegregation of all public schools, many African-American families met resistance while trying to enroll their children in all-white schools. It was no different for Mae Bertha and Matthew Carter, Mississippi sharecroppers who were determined to get their children out of the cotton fields where they themselves had worked for years.

What was different, though, was the fact that when the Carters showed up to enroll seven of their thirteen children at an all-white school in the Mississippi Delta town of Drew, they stood alone. The Carters were the only Black parents in the Sunflower County school district to take advantage of the state's new "Freedom of Choice" policy—a law that allowed parents to pick which school they wanted their children to attend.

As expected, the Carters' efforts met with strong resistance from whites. Their shack was riddled with bullets, and the plantation owner canceled their credit at his store and threw them off the plantation. At school, the children were threatened.

Undaunted, the family stood fast, relying on their faith in God for protection and each other for strength. When one of the sons considered returning to an all-Black school, his mother advised against it.

"She told me about how she and Daddy had committed themselves to the choice and how Daddy had sacrificed so many things," he said. "She never did say I couldn't change schools; she just explained things to me."

All seven Carter children finished high school and went on to graduate from the University of Mississippi.

Any decision to stand for what is right is likely to meet with some form of opposition. But when you have the courage of your convictions and a strong faith in God, you can make it through to victory.

*The LORD is the defense of my life; whom shall I dread? ... Though a host encamp against me, my heart will not fear.*

PSALM 27:1,3 NASB

On *Good Times*, the television comedy from the mid-1970s, Jimmy Walker played James (J.J.) Evans Jr., a struggling young Black artist who lived with his family in a tenement housing project in Chicago. In several episodes of the show—like "The Mural," "The Art Contest," and "Sweet Daddy Williams"—viewers got to see up close the "creative genius" portrayed by J.J. as the storylines centered on his paintings.

*The only thing that will stop you from fulfilling your dreams is you.*

But while J.J. was taking the bows on TV, the real plaudits for these extraordinary pieces of artwork were going to North Carolina artist Ernie Barnes, a former American Football League offensive guard who gave up a dream to play football to follow his true passion for painting.

"One day on the playing field, I looked up and the sun was breaking through the clouds, hitting the unmuddied areas on the uniforms, and I said, 'That's beautiful!'" Barnes once explained about his transition from the gridiron to the canvas. "I knew then that I was all over being a player. I was more interested in art. So I traded my cleats for canvas, my bruises for brushes, and put all the violence and power I had felt on the field into my paintings."

For Barnes, the ending of a football career sparked a bright new beginning that would lead to his becoming one of the most collected artists in America. Millions have been exposed to his art through *Good Times*, not to mention posters he created as the official artist for the 1984 Olympics in Los Angeles. At prices ranging in the five- and six-figure brackets, Barnes' original neomannerist paintings have been collected by some of the country's wealthiest, most famous, and powerful people.

If you realize that the dream you're pursuing does not line up with God's plan for your life, change courses. Your dream will fade, but God's plans always succeed.

*Nathan said to David, "Do all that is
in your heart, for God is with you."*
1 CHRONICLES 17:2 NASB

> True kindness presupposes the faculty
> of imagining as one's own the
> suffering and joy of others.

A nurse escorted a tired, anxious young man to the bedside of an elderly man.

"Your son is here," she whispered to the patient. She had to repeat the words several times before the patient's eyes opened. He was heavily sedated after suffering from a heart attack. He could barely see the young man standing outside the oxygen tent.

He reached out his hand, and the young man tightly wrapped his fingers around it, squeezing a message of encouragement. The nurse placed a chair next to the bedside. All through the night the young man sat holding the old man's hand and offering gentle words of hope. The dying man said nothing as he held tightly to his companion.

As dawn approached, the patient died. The young man released the lifeless hand, placed it on the bed, then went to inform the nurse. While the nurse did what was necessary, the young man waited. When she had finished her task, the nurse turned to offer her sympathy, but the young man interrupted her.

"Who was that man?" he asked.

The startled nurse replied, "I thought he was your father."

"No, he wasn't *my* father," the young man answered. "I've never seen him before in my life."

"Then why didn't you say something when I took you to him?" asked the nurse.

The young man hesitated and then replied: "When I took his hand, I realized he was too sick to see that I was not his son. I decided to stay and do my best to give him the son he so desperately needed."

There are times when others will connect with what is in your heart rather than who you are on the outside. Cherish those times. They are an expression of God's grace and mercy working through you.

*All of you should be of one mind, full of sympathy toward each other, loving one another with tender hearts and humble minds.*

1 PETER 3:8 NLT

A little boy about ten years old was standing in front of a shoe store on Broadway, barefooted, peering through the window and shivering from the cold. A lady approached the boy and asked, "My little fellow, why are you looking so earnestly in that window?"

"I was asking God to give me a pair of shoes," the boy replied.

Taking the boy by the hand, the lady walked with him into the store and asked the clerk for a half dozen pairs of socks for the boy. Then, she requested a basin of water and a towel.

Taking the little boy to the back of the store, the woman removed her gloves, knelt down, and began to wash the little boy's feet and dry them off with the towel. By this time, the clerk had returned with the six pairs of socks.

> *Poor or whatever your circumstance, you are capable of being the best of people and that best, as a human, does not come from the outside in, it comes from the inside out.*

After placing a pair of the socks on the boy's feet, the woman bought him a pair of shoes. She then tied up the remaining pairs of socks and gave them to the boy. Patting him on the head, the woman then said, "No doubt, my little fellow, you feel more comfortable now?"

As she turned to leave, the astonished boy caught her by the hand. Looking up into her face with tears in his eyes, he asked: "Are you God's wife?"

*Whoever gives to the poor will lack nothing.*
PROVERBS 28:27 NLT

> Heaven is to be
>
> at peace with things.

There once was a king who offered a prize to the artist who would paint the best picture of peace. Many artists tried. The king looked at all the pictures. But there were only two he really liked, and he had to choose between them.

One picture was of a calm lake. The lake was a perfect mirror for peaceful towering mountains all around it. Overhead was a blue sky with fluffy white clouds. All who saw this picture thought that it was a perfect picture of peace.

The other picture had mountains too. But these were rugged and bare. Above was an angry sky, from which rain fell and in which lightning played. Down the side of the mountain tumbled a foaming waterfall. This did not look peaceful at all.

But when the king looked closely, he saw a tiny bush behind the waterfall growing in a crack in the rock. In the bush a mother bird had built her nest. There, in the midst of the rush of angry water, sat the mother bird on her nest—in perfect peace.

Which picture did the king choose?

He selected the second one.

"Peace does not mean to be in a place where there is no noise, trouble, or hard work," the king later explained. "Peace means to be in the midst of all those things and still be calm in your heart. That is the real meaning of peace."

When you are looking through the eyes of God, it is easy to see peace in the midst of a storm.

*You will keep in perfect peace all who trust in you,*
*whose thoughts are fixed on you!*
ISAIAH 26:3 NLT

During Joanne's second month of nursing school, her professor gave the class a pop quiz. Joanne was a conscientious student and quickly breezed through all the questions—until she reached the last one.

"What is the first name of the woman who cleans the school?" the question read.

*Surely this is some kind of joke,* Joanne thought. She had seen the cleaning woman several times. She was tall, dark-haired, and in her fifties. But how was she supposed to know the woman's name?

Joanne handed in her paper, leaving the last question blank. Before class ended, another student asked if the last question would count toward the grade.

> Treat all people as though they were related to you.

"Absolutely," the professor responded. "In your careers you will meet many people. All are significant. They deserve your attention and care, even if all you do is smile and say hello."

Joanne missed the question that day. But she never forgot the lesson. She would also never forget

Dorothy—the cleaning woman.

What do you pay attention to the most? Maybe it's your money. Or possibly it is your relationship with others. With most people, the things that get their attention are the things that affect their lives. That is what matters most.

Your Heavenly Father, who created the heavens and earth, considers everything and everyone to be important. Even the hairs on your head, the Bible says, are important to God. Just as no one is considered small or insignificant in God's eyes, no one should be considered small in yours. Everyone counts.

*Show respect for everyone.*
*Love your Christian brothers and sisters.*
*Fear God. Show respect for the king.*
1 PETER 2:17 NLT

GLDB

## Without a rich heart,
## wealth is an ugly beggar.

One day a wealthy family man took his son on a trip to the country. He hoped to show his son how the poor country people lived.

After a stay of only one day and night at the home of a very humble man, the father and son returned home. Later, the father asked his son, "What did you think of the trip?"

"Very nice, Dad," the son replied.

"Did you notice how poor they were?" the father asked.

"Yes," his son answered.

Finally, the father wanted to know, "What did you learn?"

Looking at his father, the son responded: "I learned that we have one dog in our house, and they have four. We have a fountain in our garden, but they have a stream that has no end. We have imported lamps in our garden; they have the stars. And our garden goes to the edge of our property, but they have the entire horizon as their backyard."

Upon hearing his son's reply, the father was speechless.

Then the son said, "Thank you, Dad, for showing me how poor we really are."

Learning to be thankful for what God has done for you will help you be content with what you have, appreciating the wonders He has placed all around you.

*Remember the LORD your God, for it is he who gives you the ability to produce wealth, and so confirms his covenant, which he swore to your forefathers, as it is today.*

DEUTERONOMY 8:18

Hoping to encourage her young son's progress on the piano, a mother took the small boy to a performance by a famous pianist.

After they were seated, the mother spotted a friend in the audience and walked over to greet her. Seizing the opportunity to explore the wonders of the concert hall, the little boy rose and made his way through a door marked "No Admittance."

When the house lights dimmed and the concert was about to begin, the mother returned to her seat only to find that her son had wandered off. Suddenly, the curtains parted and spotlights focused on the impressive Steinway on stage. In horror, the mother looked to see her little boy sitting at the keyboard, innocently picking out the tune to "Twinkle, Twinkle, Little Star."

*'Tis man's to fight, but Heaven's to give success.*

At that moment, the concert pianist made his entrance. Moving quickly to the piano, he leaned over and whispered into the boy's ear, "Don't quit. Keep playing." Standing over the boy, the pianist reached down with his left hand and began filling in a bass part to the little boy's song. Soon, his right arm reached around the other side of the child and he added a running obbligato.

Together, the old master and the young novice had transformed a choppy tune into a delightful melody and a frightening situation into a creative experience.

That's the way it is with God. We try our best, but the results do not always flow so gracefully. But with the hand of the Master, our efforts can truly become a masterpiece.

*The LORD will send a blessing on …
everything you put your hand to.*
DEUTERONOMY 28:8

GLDB

> *Too many of us have a need to be*
>
> *accepted no matter what the cost.*

A story is told about a soldier who was finally coming home after having fought in Vietnam. On his way home, he called his parents from San Francisco.

"Mom and Dad, I'm coming home," he announced. "But I've got a favor to ask. I have a friend I'd like to bring with me."

"We'd love to meet him," the soldier's parents replied.

"There's something you should know," the son continued. "He was hurt pretty badly in the fighting. He stepped on a land mine and lost an arm and a leg. He has nowhere else to go, and I want him to come live with us."

"I'm sorry to hear that, son," one of the parents replied. "Maybe we can help him find somewhere to live."

"No, Mom and Dad, I want him to live with us."

"Son," said the father, "you don't know what you're asking. Someone with such a handicap would be a terrible burden on us. We have our own lives to live, and we can't let something like this interfere with our lives. I think you should just come home and forget about this guy. He'll find a way to live on his own."

Disappointed, the son hung up the phone.

Some months later, the young man's parents learned that it was their son and not his friend who had been so gravely injured.

Others may be willing to accept you based only on certain conditions, but God's love has no strings attached. He says, "I accept you unconditionally. Come as you are."

*[Jesus said,] All whom my Father gives (entrusts) to Me will come to Me; and the one who comes to Me I will most certainly not cast out [I will never, no never, reject one of them who comes to Me].*

JOHN 6:37 AMP

Dear Friend,

How are you? I just had to send a note to tell you how much I care about you. I saw you yesterday as you were talking with your friends and waited all day, hoping you would want to talk to Me too.

I gave you a sunset to close your day and a cool breeze to rest you ... and I waited, but you did not come. It hurt, but I still love you—nothing could change that. And I'm willing to wait until you want My friendship.

I saw you sleeping last night and longed to touch your brow, so I spilled the moonlight upon your face. Again I waited, wanting to rush down, so we could talk. I have so many gifts for you! You awoke and rushed off to work. My tears were in the rain.

*Communication and reconciliation introduce harmony into another's life by sensing and honoring the need to be cared for and understood.*

I long for you to hear the words of love I have for you! I try to tell you in blue skies and quiet green grass. I whisper it in the leaves on the trees and breathe it in

66

colors of flowers. I shout it to you in mountain streams and give the birds love songs to sing.

I clothe you with warm sunshine and perfume the air with nature scents. My love for you is deeper than the ocean and bigger than the biggest need in your heart!

Ask Me! Talk with Me! Don't forget Me. I have so much to share with you!

I won't hassle you any further. I've given you the freedom to choose with whom you spend your time. I will be waiting, and I will never stop loving you.


Your friend,

Jesus


*The LORD is close to all who call on him, yes, to all who call on him sincerely.*

PSALM 145:18 NLT

GLDB

Anger makes us terribly aware that something is wrong because it does not spring wantonly out of air: it has an originating cause. But anger also blinds and therefore limits and weakens: It cripples those who suffer it, and in the end those who have caused it.

There was a little boy with a bad temper. His father gave him a bag of nails, saying that every time he lost his temper he was to hammer a nail into the back fence.

The first day the boy had driven thirty-seven nails into the fence. Then, the number started to gradually decrease. The boy discovered it was easier to hold his temper than it was to drive nails into the fence.

Finally, the day came when the boy did not lose his temper at all. His father then suggested that the boy pull out one nail from the fence for each day that he was able to hold his temper.

The days passed, and the young boy was finally able to tell his father that all the nails were gone.

The father took his son by the hand and led him to the fence.

"You have done well, son," he told the boy. "But look at the holes in the fence. The fence will never be the same. When you say things in anger, they leave a scar just like this one. You can put a knife into a man and draw it out, but it won't matter how many times you say, 'I'm sorry.' The wound will still be there. A verbal wound is as bad as a physical one."

Wounds may heal, but the scars they cause often remain forever. Committing your words and actions to God can help you avoid speaking words that you can't take back or inflicting injuries that may never heal.

*Don't be quick-tempered,*
*for anger is the friend of fools.*
ECCLESIASTES 7:9 NLT

On January 14, 1969, the late comedian Red Skelton touched the hearts of millions of Americans with his commentary on the Pledge of Allegiance, which was read on *The Red Skelton Hour* television program. Before reading, Skelton explained that the version had come from his former schoolteacher Mr. Lasswell, who one day said to his class:

> *He loves his country best who strives to make it best.*

"I've been listening to you boys and girls recite the Pledge of Allegiance all semester, and it seems as though it is becoming monotonous to you. If I may, I'd like to recite it and try to explain to you the meaning of each word."

The following is the version put forth by that teacher:

I—*me, an individual, a committee of one.*

Pledge—*dedicate all of my worldly goods, to give without self-pity.*

Allegiance—*my love and my devotion.*

To the flag—*our standard, Old Glory, a symbol of freedom. Wherever she waves, there's respect because your loyalty has given her a dignity that shouts freedom is everybody's job!*

Of the United—*that means that we have all come together.*

States of America—*individual communities that have united into forty-eight great states. Forty-eight individual communities with pride and dignity and purpose, all divided with imaginary boundaries, yet united to a common purpose—and that's love for country.*

And to the republic for which it stands—*a state in which sovereign power is invested in representatives chosen by the people to govern. And government is the people and it's from the people to the leaders, not from the leaders to the people.*

One nation ... under God—*meaning "so blessed by God."*

Indivisible—*incapable of being divided.*

With liberty—*which is freedom—the right of power to live one's own life without threats, fear or some sort of retaliation.*

And justice—*the principle or quality of dealing fairly with others.*

For all—*which means, boys and girls, it's as much your country as it is mine.*

*This version of the Pledge of Allegiance has been twice read into the Congressional Record of the United States and has received numerous awards.*

*Uprightness and right standing with God (moral and spiritual rectitude in every area and relation) elevate a nation, but sin is a reproach to any people.*
PROVERBS 14:34 AMP

> Struggle is strengthening.
> Battling with evil gives us the power
> to battle evil even more.

A man sat watching as a butterfly struggled to make its way through the tiny hole of its cocoon. Sensing the butterfly might be in trouble, the man decided to help.

Taking a pair of scissors, the man began to snip away at the cocoon, and soon the butterfly was free. But the man noticed something. The butterfly had a swollen body and small, shriveled wings.

The man watched with curiosity, expecting the creature's wings to enlarge and expand at any moment in order to support its body. But nothing happened. The butterfly was doomed to spend the rest of its life crawling around with a swollen body and shriveled up wings. It was never able to fly.

Through his eagerness to help the creature, the man did not understand that what he had witnessed from the beginning was part of the butterfly's developmental process. The restriction of the cocoon and the struggle required for the butterfly to get through the tiny opening is God's way of forcing fluid from the body of the butterfly into its wings to prepare it for flight.

Sometimes struggles are necessary if we are to grow in spiritual things. God may allow us to face tough challenges, but He always provides a way to get through them.

*Fight the good fight of the faith.*
1 TIMOTHY 6:12

A man who hired a carpenter to help restore an old farmhouse gave this account of the first day of work and a tremendous transformation that he witnessed.

"The carpenter had just finished a rough first day on the job," the man recalled.

"A flat tire made him lose an hour of work, his electric saw quit, and his truck wouldn't start. While I drove him home, he sat in stone silence. On arriving, he invited me in to meet his family. As we walked toward the front door, he paused briefly at a small tree, touching the tips of the branches with both hands.

"After opening the door, he underwent an amazing transformation. His tanned face was wreathed in smiles, and he hugged his two small children and gave his wife a kiss. Afterward, he walked me to my car. We passed the tree, and my curiosity got the better of me. I asked him about what I had seen him do earlier. His response was very revealing:

> *There is nothing written in the Bible, Old or New Testament, that says, "If you believe in Me, you ain't going to have no troubles."*

"'Oh, that's my trouble tree,' he replied. 'I know I can't help having troubles on the job, but one thing's for sure; troubles don't belong in the house with my wife and the children. So I just hang them up on the tree every night when I come home. Then in the morning, I pick them up again.

"'Funny thing is,' he said, 'when I come out in the morning to pick them up, there aren't nearly as many as I remember hanging up the night before.'"

Hanging up your troubles should not be like hanging up a hat. You might need that hat again, but there is no need to continue carrying around troubles. Give them to God instead. He promises to take them away—forever!

*[God] has delivered me from all my troubles, and my eyes have looked in triumph on my foes.*
PSALM 54:7

> Humility is the most difficult of all virtues to achieve; nothing dies harder than the desire to think well of oneself.

Capt. Charles Plumb, a jet pilot in Vietnam, had flown seventy-five combat missions before his plane was shot down. Plumb ejected and parachuted into enemy hands and was held captive for six years.

Surviving the ordeal, Plumb returned to the United States and eventually lectured on lessons learned from his experience. One day while dining with his wife in a restaurant, a man came up and said, "You're Plumb! You flew jet fighters in Vietnam from the aircraft carrier *Kitty Hawk*. You were shot down!"

Astonished at being recognized, Plumb asked, "How in the world did you know that?"

"I packed your parachute," the man answered.

Plumb gasped in surprise.

"I guess it worked!" the man said.

"It sure did," Plumb assured him. "If that chute hadn't worked, I wouldn't be here today."

Plumb could not sleep that night for thinking about that man.

"I kept wondering what he might have looked like in a Navy uniform: a white hat, a bib in the back, and bell bottom trousers. I wonder how many times I might have seen him and not even said, 'Good morning,' because, you see, I was a fighter pilot, and he was 'just a sailor.'"

Plumb also thought of the many hours the sailor had spent, working on a long wooden table in the bowels of the ship, carefully weaving the shrouds and folding the silks of each chute. Did he realize that each time he did this he held in his hands the fate of someone he didn't even know?

Through a chance encounter, Plumb came to realize what all should know—that everyone has someone who provides for them in some way. The world might call them the "little people," but in reality they are big in God's sight. Do you know who's packing your parachute?

*If you don't brag about the good you do,*
*then you will be truly wise!*
JAMES 3:13 NLT

Two brothers who lived on adjoining land had fallen into a conflict that resulted in weeks of silence. One morning a man holding a toolbox knocked at John's door.

"I'm looking for a few days' work," the man said. "Do you, perhaps, have a few small jobs here and there that I could help with?"

"I do have a job for you," John answered. "Look across the creek at that farm. That's my neighbor's. In fact, it's my younger brother's. Last week there was a meadow between us. He took his bulldozer to the river levee, and now there is a creek between us. Well, he may have done this to spite me, but I'll do him one better.

"See that pile of lumber by the barn? I want you to build me a fence, so I won't need to see his place or his face anymore."

"I think I understand the situation," the carpenter responded.

John went off to town, and the carpenter went to work.

> Let us
>
> have peace.

Upon his return, John was surprised to find that the carpenter had not built a fence. Instead, John looked to see a bridge stretching from one side of the creek to the other and his brother coming toward them with his hand outstretched.

"You are quite a fellow to build this bridge after all I've said and done," the younger brother said.

The two brothers met in the middle, taking each other by the hand. They turned to see the carpenter hoist his toolbox onto his shoulder.

"Stay a few days," the older brother invited. "I've a lot of other projects for you."

"I'd love to stay on," the carpenter answered, "but I have many more bridges to build."

Relationships are easier to maintain when your Heavenly Father is involved. You can trust Him to give you the strength and peace to weather any storm that might arise through disagreements or misunderstandings.

*You will be called Repairer of Broken Walls,*
*Restorer of Streets with Dwellings.*
ISAIAH 58:12

GLDB

## When I pray,
## my heart is in my prayer.

Think of the acronym "ASAP" and almost immediately you think *hurry*. That's what life today is like: everything has to be done "As Soon As Possible." But what if the acronym stood for something that involved less stress, less tension, less immediacy. Here are some thoughts:

There is work to do, deadlines to meet;
you've got no time to spare.
But as you hurry and scurry,
Always Say A Prayer.

In the midst of family chaos, quality time is rare.
Do your best; let God do the rest; and
Always Say A Prayer.

It may seem like your worries are more
than you can bear.

Slow down and take a breather; and

Always Say A Prayer.

God knows how stressful life is.
He wants to ease our cares.
He'll respond to all your needs if you

Always Say A Prayer.

Who says everything has to be done "As Soon as Possible"? Life within itself is a challenge, but God has given it to us to enjoy. The challenges that come with day-to-day life are much easier to bear when you approach each one by saying a prayer.

What are you facing today? Whatever it is, with God you can handle it. Instead of being stressed by the rigors of life, take life slowly. Take time to pray about each situation, and then let God show you the best way to handle it.

*Pray without ceasing.*
1 THESSALONIANS 5:17 NASB

A sportswriter was invited to dinner at the residence of golfing legend Arnold Palmer. He arrived a bit early and was greeted by Palmer's wife, who said her husband would be down in a moment.

While waiting, the writer asked to see Palmer's trophy room.

"Oh, we don't have a trophy room," Mrs. Palmer replied.

Later, the writer asked the professional golfer why he didn't have a place to show off his trophies, which represented more than ninety tour victories, including several major tournaments.

*I'm into now and the future.*

Palmer looked the columnist in the eye and replied, "For what? That's yesterday's news!" Then, the golf legend explained:

"I have enjoyed every victory and cherished the memories. I have celebrated those tournaments. But come Monday morning of the next week, I'm no different from the man who missed the cut last week. In fact, he is probably hungrier for a victory than I am.

"So if I am to be competitively ready, I must get

my thoughts off yesterday and deal with today. Someday I'll take the time to look back. But as long as I want to stay competitive, I must never stop and marvel at what I have accomplished, only look forward to the challenge at hand."

Instead of living with yesterday's victories, think about what God has in store for your tomorrows. His plan is for you to always be successful.

*I am still not all I should be, but I am focusing all my energies on this one thing: Forgetting the past and looking forward to what lies ahead, I strain to reach the end of the race and receive the prize for which God, through Christ Jesus, is calling us up to heaven.*

PHILIPPIANS 3:13-14 NLT

> Marriage is the proper remedy.
> It is the most natural state of man, and
> therefore the state in which you will
> find solid happiness.

BLESSED ... are the husband and wife who continue to be affectionate and considerate, showing love after the wedding bells have ceased ringing.

BLESSED ... are the husband and wife who are as polite and courteous to one another as they are to their friends.

BLESSED ... are the husband and wife who have a sense of humor, for this attribute will be a handy shock absorber.

BLESSED ... are the husband and wife who love each other more than any other person in the world and joyfully fulfill their marriage vows—a lifetime of fidelity and mutual helpfulness.

BLESSED ... are the husband and wife who attain parenthood, for children are a heritage of the Lord.

BLESSED ... are the husband and wife who remember to thank God for their food before they partake of it and set apart some time each day for reading the Bible and prayer.

BLESSED … are the husband and wife who never speak loudly to one another but make their home a place "where seldom is heard a discouraging word."

BLESSED … are the husband and wife who faithfully attend a Christ-filled church and work together for the advancement of Christ's kingdom.

BLESSED … are the husband and wife who can work out the adjustments in their marriage without interference from relatives.

BLESSED … are the husband and wife who take the time to fully understand financial matters and have worked out a true partnership when it comes to the management of money.

BLESSED … are the husband and wife who humbly dedicate their lives and home to Christ and practice the teachings of Christ by being selfless, loyal, and loving.

*Let marriage be held in honor (esteemed worthy,*
*precious, of great price, and especially dear)*
*in all things.*
HEBREWS 13:4 AMP

Several years ago a preacher moved to Houston, Texas. Some weeks after he arrived, he had occasion to ride the bus from his home to the downtown area. When he sat down, he discovered that the driver had accidentally given him a quarter too much change.

As he considered what to do, he thought, *I should return the quarter; it would be wrong to keep it.* But then he had another thought: *Oh, who cares; it's only a quarter. Who would worry about this small amount?* The bus company won't miss it. *They already charge too high a fare. I'll just keep it and consider it a gift from the Lord.*

When the preacher reached his destination, he paused momentarily at the door and handed the quarter to the driver. "You gave me too much change," he said.

> Never give in, never, never, never—in nothing great or small, large or petty—never give in—except in convictions of honor and good sense.

"Aren't you the new preacher in town?" the driver asked. "I have a confession to make. I've been thinking lately about going to worship somewhere, and I just wanted to see what you would do if I gave you too much change."

Stepping down from the bus, the preacher grabbed hold of the nearest light pole, balanced himself, and said: "Oh, Lord, I almost sold Your Son for a quarter."

Jesus paid the ultimate price for your salvation. Guard it with your life, rather than your pocketbook.

*Do not use dishonest standards when measuring length, weight, or volume. Your scales and weights must be accurate. Your containers for measuring dry goods or liquids must be accurate.*

LEVITICUS 19:35-36 NLT

GLDB

## The mother's heart is
## the child's schoolroom.

A man stopped at a flower shop to have some flowers wired to his mother, who lived two hundred miles away. As he got out of his car, he noticed a young girl sitting on the curb sobbing.

"What's the matter?" he asked the girl.

She looked up at the man and replied, "I wanted to buy a red rose for my mother. But I only have seventy-five cents, and a rose costs two dollars."

"Come on in with me," the man smiled and said. "I'll buy you a rose."

Once inside the store, the man bought the little girl a rose for her mother and ordered some for his own. As they were leaving the shop, he offered the girl a ride home.

"Thank you," she exclaimed. "You can take me to my mother."

The young girl then directed the man to drive to a

cemetery, where she placed the rose on a freshly dug grave. The man returned to the flower shop, cancelled the wire order, picked up a bouquet, and drove the two hundred miles to his mother's house.

God's love for you is so special that He made sure that distance would never keep you from communicating with Him. His Holy Spirit is your connection.

How are the relationships between your loved ones and you? If miles of separation have kept you from sharing your love for them, close the gap. Pay them a visit, and let them know how you feel. Give them their flowers while they can still smell them—and do it in person.

*Pay close attention, friend, to what your father tells you; never forget what you learned at your mother's knee.*

PROVERBS 1:8 MSG

Walking home from school one day, Mark noticed the boy ahead of him had tripped and dropped all his belongings—books, two sweaters, a baseball bat, a glove, and a small tape recorder. Mark knelt down and helped the boy pick up the scattered articles.

As they walked, Mark and the boy, whose name was Bill, discovered they each enjoyed some of the same things, including video games, baseball, and history. Bill also told Mark that he had just broken up with his girlfriend.

*His daily prayer, far better understood in acts than words, was simply doing good.*

The two continued to see each other around school, and on occasion they had lunch together. After graduating from junior high school, Mark and Bill ended up at the same high school, where they again had contact through the years.

Finally, the long-awaited senior year arrived. Three weeks before graduation, Bill asked Mark if they could talk. Bill reminded him of the day they first met so many years before.

"Have you ever wondered why I was carrying so

many things from school that day?" asked Bill. "You see, I cleaned out my locker because I didn't want to leave a mess for anyone else. I had hidden some of my mother's pills, and I was going home to commit suicide. But after we spent some time together that day, I realized I didn't want to miss out on our friendship. It gave me something to live for. So you see, Mark, when you picked up my books for me that day, you saved my life."

You may think the kindness you show others means nothing, but often you have been hand picked by God to speak something special into someone's life. Welcome every opportunity to let God use your voice to bless others.

*[Jesus said,] "Let your good deeds shine out for all to see, so that everyone will praise your heavenly Father."*
MATTHEW 5:16 NLT

> Every man is born into the world to do something
> unique and something distinctive, and if he or she
> does not do it, it will never be done. If Lincoln had
> not emancipated the slaves, if Lincoln had not
> delivered those words in his inaugural address,
> those words would never have been written.

There were two warring tribes in the Andes—one that lived in the lowlands, the other high in the mountains. One day, the mountain people invaded the lowlanders. As they were plundering the village, they found a baby and took it with them when they returned to the mountains.

The lowlanders didn't know how to climb the mountains. They didn't know any of the trails the mountain people used and had no idea how to track them in the steep terrain. Still, they sent out their best fighting men to climb the mountains and bring the baby home.

The men tried one method of climbing and then another. They tried one trail and then another. After several days of effort, however, they had climbed only several hundred feet. Discouraged and disappointed, the lowlander men decided the cause was lost and prepared to return to their village below.

As they were packing their gear for the descent, they were amazed to see the baby's mother walking toward them. She was coming down the mountain—the one they had been unable to climb—with her baby strapped to her back.

The astonished men ran to greet her. "How did you get up the mountain?" they asked. "We are the strongest and most capable men in the village, and we couldn't find a way up the mountain."

The mother looked at them, shrugged her shoulders, and said, "It wasn't your baby."

The woman was motivated by her great love for her child. For her, failure was not an option.

When you undertake a challenge, ask God to set it deep in your heart, make it a passion that burns inside you. That's a key to making the impossible—possible!

*Remember that in a race everyone runs, but only one person gets the prize. You also must run in such a way that you will win. ... So I run straight to the goal with purpose in every step.*
1 Corinthians 9:24,26 nlt

A small boy approached his slightly older sister with a question.

"Susie," he asked, "can anybody see God?"

Busy with other things, Susie curtly replied, "Of course not, silly. God is so far up in Heaven that nobody can see Him."

Time passed, but his question still lingered. So the boy approached his mom.

"Mom, can anybody see God?"

"No, not really," she gently answered. "God is a spirit, and He dwells in our hearts, but we can't really see Him."

Somewhat satisfied but still wondering, the youngster went on his way. Not long afterward, his saintly old grandfather took the little boy on a fishing trip. They were having a great time together. The sun was beginning to set with unusual splendor, and the grandfather stared silently at the exquisite beauty unfolding before them.

> People sat around on the porch and passed around the pictures of their thoughts for others to look at and see.

On seeing the face of his grandfather reflecting such deep peace and contentment, the little boy thought for a moment and finally spoke hesitantly.

"Granddad, I wasn't going to ask anybody else, but I wonder if you can tell me the answer to something I've been wondering about for a long time. Can anybody really see God?"

The old man did not even turn his head. A long moment passed before he answered.

"Son," he said quietly, "it's getting so I can't see anything else."

When you want to see God, you must look with the eyes of your heart.

*You will seek me and find me*
*when you seek me with all your heart.*
JEREMIAH 29:13

> *The only things we ever keep*
>
> *are what we give away.*

A son and his father were walking along a mountain ridge when the son suddenly stumbled and hurt himself. As he fell forward, he screamed, "AAAhhhhhhhhhhh!"

To his surprise, he heard someone return his "AAAhhhhhhhhhhh!" from somewhere deep in the mountain.

Curious as to the source of the voice, the son yelled, "Who are you?"

Instantly, he received the answer: "Who are you?"

Angered at the response, the son screamed out, "Coward!"

The voice came back, "Coward!"

The son looked at his father and said, "What's going on?"

The father smiled and said, "Pay attention, my son."

He then screamed to the mountain, "I admire you!"

The voice answered, "I admire you!"

Again the man screamed, "You are a champion!"

And again the voice answered, "You are a champion!"

The son was surprised, but still didn't understand, so the father explained.

"People call this an *echo*, but really this is *life*," he said. "It gives you back everything you say or do. Our lives are simply reflections of our actions. If you want more love in the world, create more love in your heart. If you want those around you to be more positive, be more positive yourself. This relationship applies to everything, in all aspects of life. Life will give you back what you have given to it."

This principle is called the "doctrine of reciprocity." Be sure that you are sending forth good things, godly words and actions into the lives of others. Then watch as God sends them bouncing right back to you.

*Whatever a man sows, that and that only is what*
*he will reap. And let us not lose heart and grow*
*weary and faint in acting nobly and doing right,*
*for in due time and at the appointed season*
*we shall reap, if we do not loosen and*
*relax our courage and faint.*

GALATIANS 6:7,9 AMP

There is an old Chinese tale about a woman whose only son died. In her grief, she went to the holy man and asked, "What prayers, what magical incantations do you have to bring my son back to life?"

Instead of sending her away or reasoning with her, the holy man said to her, "Fetch me a mustard seed from a home that has never known sorrow. We will use it to drive the sorrow out of your life."

The woman went off at once in search of that magical mustard seed.

She went first to a splendid mansion, knocked at the door, and said, "I am looking for a home that has never known sorrow. Is this such a place? It is very important to me."

*Self-sacrifice is the real miracle out of which all the reported miracles grew.*

"You've certainly come to the wrong place," the woman was told by the occupants, who began to describe all the tragic things that had befallen them in their lives.

The woman thought to herself, *Who is better able to*

*help these poor, unfortunate people than I, who have had misfortune of my own?* She stayed to comfort them, then went on in search of a home that had never known sorrow.

But wherever she turned, she found one tale after another of sadness and misfortune. She became so involved in ministering to other people's grief that ultimately she forgot about her quest for the magical mustard seed, never realizing that her concern for others had, in fact, driven the sorrow out of her own life.

When you allow God to use you to comfort and encourage others who are going through a difficult time, you will see the worry and anxiety of your own problems vanishing like a vapor.

*As we have opportunity, let us do good to all,*
*especially to those who are of the household of faith.*
GALATIANS 6:10 NKJV

> When Napoleon was winning battles
> he was loved by his people, but when he lost,
> he lost his friends. I want my friends to
> love me if I lose or win a battle
> tomorrow or a year hence.

It was Friday morning, and a young businessman finally decided to ask his boss for a raise. Before leaving for work, he told his wife what he was about to do. All day long he felt nervous and apprehensive. Finally in the late afternoon, he summoned the courage to approach his employer, and to his delight, the boss agreed to the raise.

The elated husband arrived home to a beautiful table set with their best china and glowing candles. Smelling the aroma of a festive meal, he figured that someone from the office had called his wife and tipped her off.

Finding her in the kitchen, he eagerly shared the details of his good news. They embraced and danced around the room before sitting down to the wonderful meal his wife had prepared.

Next to his plate, the husband found an artistically lettered note that read, "Congratulations, darling! I knew you'd get the raise! This dinner is to show you how much I love you."

Later, while on his way into the kitchen to help his wife serve dessert, the husband noticed that a second card had fallen from her pocket. Picking it up off the floor, he read: "Don't worry about not getting the raise! It's just a matter of time, because you deserve it! This dinner is to show you how much I love you."

Love that is unconditional works under any circumstance. It is how God responds to us and how we should respond to others.

*Love never gives up. Love cares more for others than for self. Love ... trusts God always, always looks for the best, never looks back, but keeps going to the end.*
1 CORINTHIANS 13:4,7 MSG

A young boy rushed into a service station and asked the manager if he had a pay phone. The manager nodded, "Sure, over there."

The boy dropped in a couple of coins, dialed a number, and waited for an answer.

Finally, someone came on the line.

"Uh, sir," the boy said in a deep voice, "could you use an honest, hardworking young man to work for you?"

The station manager could not help overhearing the question. After a moment or two the boy said, "Oh, you already have an honest, hardworking young man? Well, okay. Thanks just the same."

> He that hath a trade hath an estate; he that hath a calling hath an office of profit and honor.

With a broad smile stretched across his face, the boy hung up the phone and started back to his car, humming and obviously elated.

"Hey, just a minute!" the station manager called after him. "I couldn't help but hear your conversation. Why are you so happy? I thought the guy said he already had somebody and didn't need you?"

The young man smiled. "Well, you see, I am the honest, hardworking young man. I was just checking up on my job!"

When you want to know where you stand in life, ask God. He keeps accurate records and doesn't mind sharing His notes with you.

*The fire will test the quality of each man's work.*
*If what he has built survives,*
*he will receive his reward.*

1 CORINTHIANS 3:13-14

GLDB

Let not the shining thread of hope become so enmeshed in the web of circumstance that we lose sight of it.

## ABC's to Live By

Although things are not perfect
Because of trial or pain,
Continue in thanksgiving and
Do not begin to blame.
Even when the times are hard,
Fierce winds are bound to blow.
God is forever able.
Hold on to what you know.
Imagine life without His love.
Joy would cease to be.
Keep thanking Him for all the things
Love imparts to thee.
Move out of "Camp Complaining."

No weapon that is known
On earth can yield the power
Praise can do alone.
Quit looking at the future.
Redeem the time at hand.
Start every day with worship.
To "thank" is a command.
Until we see Him coming
Victorious in the sky,
We'll run the race with gratitude
Xalting God most high.
Yes, there'll be good times and yes, some will be bad, but
Zion waits in glory—where none are ever sad!

*I am counting on the LORD; yes, I am counting on
him. I have put my hope in his word. …
O Israel, hope in the LORD; for with the LORD
there is unfailing love and an overflowing
supply of salvation.*
PSALM 130:5,7 NLT

Though Althea Gibson longed to become somebody, living in an impoverished home in Harlem gave her little reason to believe that could ever happen. A restless youngster with no interest in school, Gibson looked to the streets for solace but found none.

By the time she was fourteen, the rebellious teenager had already been labeled a truant. Since she was a ward of the New York City Welfare Department, social workers reached out to Gibson and eventually steered her into the local Police Athletic League sports programs.

It was a move that would eventually turn Gibson's life around.

Through the league, Gibson learned to play paddle tennis—a skill that led to tennis lessons at an exclusive all-Black club in Harlem. Later, as a member of the Harlem River Tennis Courts, Gibson won the annual American Tennis Association's New York State Tournament thirteen times.

> Not in the clamor of the crowded street,
> Not in the shouts and plaudits of the throng,
> But in ourselves, are triumph and defeat.

Gibson was encouraged by two Black doctors, who offered to help her advance if she would return to school and get her education. While living in the Virginia home of one of the doctors, Gibson attended public school and practiced on the family's private tennis court. After graduating tenth in her class, Gibson accepted a tennis scholarship to Florida Agricultural and Mechanical University in Tallahassee.

Though successful, Gibson found no solace in the fact that she played only in all-Black tournaments. That changed in 1950, when a white tennis player noted in *American Lawn Tennis* magazine that bigotry had kept Gibson out of major competitions.

Over the next several years, Gibson would win fifty-six singles and doubles titles and gain international acclaim as the first African American to win championships at grand slam tournaments such as Wimbledon, the French Open, the Australian Doubles, and the United States Open.

God will always give you opportunities to develop the gifts and talents He's placed in your life. He expects you to watch for the open doors He provides and to be willing to walk through them.

*As he thinks within himself, so he is.*

PROVERBS 23:7 NASB

> The greatest grace of a gift,
> perhaps, is that it anticipates and
> admits of no return.

Robert Walter Johnson was a physician whose care for others went far beyond tending the physical body. Johnson had a personal concern that people, and particularly those of his own African-American race, be given the chance to utilize their talents and skills.

While much about the doctor's private life may not be known, a video titled: *Dr. R. Walter "Whirlwind" Johnson: The Legacy of a Life of Service to Others* offers a good picture of the humanitarian side of this Lynchburg, Virginia, physician and his contributions to others through the sport of tennis.

A tennis player himself, Johnson was aware of the obstacles faced by most promising young Black tennis players of not having a place to practice. Johnson's concern led him to construct a tennis court in his own backyard in Lynchburg and then open it up to a number of young players. He spent part of his summers during the 1940s and '50s training students and helping them develop their skills.

Among his students were a very young Althea Gibson and a tall, lanky kid named Arthur Ashe. They would one day become the first African-American male and female players to win Wimbledon titles.

Johnson, who also instilled into his young students the importance of perseverance, hard work, self-respect, and self-discipline, was known for his military style of instruction and discipline, always stressing his special code of sportsmanship: deference, sharp appearance, and no cheating at any time.

Not everyone is destined to play out success in the spotlight. Helping others reach their God-given potential is a gift and calling in itself.

*The company of believers was of one heart and soul, and not one of them claimed that anything which he possessed was [exclusively] his own, but everything they had was in common and for the use of all.*

ACTS 4:32 AMP

In his book, *Roots*, American author, biographer, and scriptwriter Alex Haley gives an account of the birth of his ancestor, Kunta Kinte, noting how the infant's grandmother, Yaisa, laughed with joy as she witnessed the birth of the firstborn boy of her son Omoro and his wife, Binta. Several days later, during the naming ceremonies, the Alimano prayed over the infant, entreating deity to grant the child long life and success in bringing credit and pride and many children to his family, his village, and his tribe. They also prayed for the child to receive the strength and spirit needed to preserve and bring honor to the name he was about to receive.

> Navies nor armies can exalt the state ... but one great man can make a country great.

Names, it appears, were not mere words when it came to ancient tribes of Africa. The ancestors believed that the name contained secrets of the child's existence and defined the challenges to be overcome in the future.

Haley described the seriousness of Omoro and Binta's ritual of naming their child:

"By ancient customs, for the next seven days there was but a single task with which Omoro would seriously occupy himself, the selection of a name for his firstborn son. It would have to be a name rich with history and promise, for the people of his tribe—the Mandinkan—believed that a child would develop seven of the characteristics of whomever or whatever he was named for."

Once a child was named, he was identified and accepted as a member of the village.

Similarly, when you become a Christian your name is changed and takes on new meaning. Not only are you a member of a brand-new family but also your new name is recorded in God's Book of Life.

*You will be called by a new name which the mouth of the LORD will designate.*
ISAIAH 62:2 NASB

GLDB

> *The only way of finding the limits of the possible is by going beyond them into the impossible.*

Were it not for the encouragement of his mother, Joe might have easily given up on his future and considered himself a failure. All the signs were there. He was kept back in the first grade and diagnosed by doctors as being mentally retarded. The youngster even suffered a severe speech impediment, which made it difficult for him to communicate with others.

But the love and faith of a mother who envisioned her son as someday being a role model for others were stronger than all the negative signs displayed in his life.

"When I was born, 14 of us (12 children and 2 parents) lived in a shack," Joe Dudley Sr. would later explain about his rise from poverty to becoming one of the wealthiest African Americans in the country. "I promised God that if He helped me make it, I would spend my life helping other people—not just my family but people in general. We must make a contribution in the world. My people, African Americans, need more help than many others."

More than twenty-five years later and keeping the promise that he made to God, Joe Dudley is the CEO of Dudley Products, a multi-million-dollar cosmetics and hair care company in Kernersville, North Carolina. Along with his wife, Eunice, Dudley works out of their eight-thousand-square-foot corporate office, overseeing the manufacture and distribution of more than 120 professional and retail hair care products and personal care cosmetics. These products are shipped directly to cosmetologists and barbers in forty states and overseas.

In addition, Dudley encourages others through motivational speeches and a series of books he has written, encouraging others that if he could be successful, so can they.

Handicaps do not have to be a stumbling block to success. Through faith in God and faith in yourself, all things are within your grasp. Take hold and go for the gold!

*Jesus said, … All things can be (are possible) to him who believes!*
MARK 9:23 AMP

Singer Chuck Berry—whose credits include such popular tunes from the 1950s and '60s as *Maybellene, Roll Over Beethoven,* and *Johnny B. Goode*—has the distinction of being recognized by most as the "father of rock and roll." One accolade rarely mentioned is that Berry was the creator of the famous "duck walk."

In his autobiography, Berry explained how this entertaining part of his performance, which eventually became his trademark, came into being.

*Creativity is seeing something that doesn't exist already. You need to find out how you can bring it into being and that way be a playmate with God.*

"A brighter seat of my memories is based on pursuing my rubber ball," he wrote. "Once it happened to bounce under the kitchen table, and I was trying to retrieve it while it was still bouncing. Usually I was reprimanded for disturbing activities when there was company in the house, as there was then. But this time my manner of retrieving the ball created a big laugh from Mother's choir members. Stooping with full-bended knees, but with my back and head vertical, I fit under the tabletop while scooting forward reaching for the ball.

"This squatting manner was requested by members of the family many times thereafter for the entertainment of visitors, and soon, from their appreciation and encouragement, I looked forward to the ritual. An act was in the making. After it had been abandoned for years, I happened to remember the maneuver while performing in New York for the first time and some journalist branded it the 'duck walk.'"

God's creative genius can be seen in all things great and small—even the unique characteristics God has placed in each and every human being.

*Your beginnings will seem humble,*
*so prosperous will your future be.*
Job 8:7

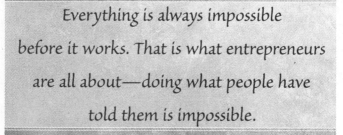

> Everything is always impossible before it works. That is what entrepreneurs are all about—doing what people have told them is impossible.

As one of thirteen children growing up on a small farm in East Texas, a young Bessie Coleman was eager to learn and eventually was able to earn enough money to pay for her secondary education and start college. When the money ran out and she was forced to return to Texas and work as a laundress, she could have given up on her dreams and ambitions. But that didn't happen. The tenacious young woman had vowed that one day she would "amount to something."

What was the "something" Coleman aspired to? Though it was a rarity among women and virtually nonexistent for Black women, she was determined to become an aviator. Ignoring all the obstacles created by her sex and race, Coleman set out to achieve her goal. When she was snubbed in the United States, Coleman saved her hard-earned money and traveled to France, where race was less of a barrier.

In June of 1921, after completing seven months of

instruction and a rigorous qualifying exam, she received her license from the Federation Aeronautique Internationale, the first Black woman in the institution's history to do so. Two months later, aviatrix Coleman returned to the United States where, as the first African American to earn an international pilot's license, she would enjoy a brief yet distinguished career as a performance flier. Her pioneering achievements served as an inspiration for a generation of African-American men and women.

Your ability to break down any barrier begins with the knowledge that God has given you strength and He calls you an overcomer. Think about what He has already brought you through; then let that encourage you to take on any new challenge that comes your way.

*Jesus looked at them and said, With men this is impossible, but all things are possible with God.*
MATTHEW 19:26 AMP

In her foreword, former first lady Eleanor Roosevelt suggested that the book *The Long Shadow of Little Rock* "should shock the conscience of America and bring a realization of where we stand in the year 1962 in these United States."

The book recounts the plight of nine Black students who, in 1957, took a stand against the segregation of public schools by becoming the first of their race to attend Central High School in Little Rock, Arkansas. But the memoir affords an even more telling history of the life and struggles of Daisy Bates, the civil-rights pioneer who stood at the center of the historic event, serving as an advisor and mentor to the students who would later become known as "The Little Rock Nine."

> Man is unjust, but God is just; and finally justice triumphs.

For Bates, the fact that Blacks living in 1957 could be kept from attending the school of their choice and thus denied a quality education was just one more reminder that nothing had changed since her first encounter with racism as a child of seven. Bates had gone to the store for her mother to buy some meat when the butcher told her: "Niggers have to wait 'til I wait on the white people."

"I knew I was a Negro, but I did not really understand what that meant until I was seven years old," Bates would later write of the encounter.

There would be no more "waiting," Bates had decided upon taking up the cause of these young students. On September 25, 1957, the nine students entered the school under the protection of military guard sent to Little Rock by President Dwight D. Eisenhower. In May 1958, following its first year of integration, Central High graduated its first African-American student.

When you feel strongly about a matter, make sure those feelings are supported by God's Word. Then you can take action knowing you have the backing of Him who promises to always be with you and never leave.

*God does not show favoritism.*
ROMANS 2:11

> We're fighting for the right to be
> different and not be punished for it.
> Equal means sameness.

Spurned by members of her own race because she lacked social and athletic abilities, was light-skinned, and had a good grade of hair, Gwendolyn Brooks turned to her family for love and comfort. The youngster also found great solace in reading books and writing. She composed her first poem at the age of seven.

By the time she was eleven, young Gwendolyn was regularly making entries of her thoughts in a notebook and by age seventeen had published more than seventy-five poems. Her parents, who supported her efforts, even excused their daughter from some of her household chores and set up a desk where she could work.

"I felt that I had to write," Brooks would later explain about her aptitude for being creative. "Even if I had never been published, I knew I would go on writing, enjoying it, and experiencing the challenge."

The challenge of writing led to a number of honors for Brooks. In 1945, a collection of her poems—in which Brooks chronicles the everyday lives, aspirations, and disappointments of ordinary Black Americans— was released to critical acclaim under the title *A Street in Bronzeville*. Perhaps her greatest honor came five years later when she was awarded the Pulitzer Prize for *Annie Allen*, a book-length poem about a Black girl's road to womanhood. She was the first Black writer ever to receive the prestigious award.

Being rejected by those around you is no reason to believe you will never amount to anything. Often, rejection frees you up to explore those areas God has mapped out for you.

*The LORD will not reject his people;*
*he will never forsake his inheritance.*
PSALM 94:14

In April 1896, educator Booker T. Washington made George Washington Carver an offer the world would be glad he did not refuse.

"I cannot offer you money, position, or fame," Washington told Carver upon proposing he take the position of director of the Department of Agricultural Research at Tuskegee Norman and Industrial Institute in Alabama. "The first two you have. The last, from the position you now occupy, you will no doubt achieve. ... I offer you in their place: work—hard, hard work, the task of bringing a people from degradation, poverty, and waste to full manhood. Your department exists only on paper, and your laboratory will have to be in your head."

*To be successful, grow to the point where you completely forget yourself; that is, to lose yourself in a great cause.*

Washington may have seen something in Carver that was not yet obvious to others. But it would not be long before the world would hear about Carver and benefit richly from the vast knowledge of a man who began life as a slave, was kidnapped by night riders, and was ransomed for a $300 racehorse.

As a chemist and director of the Department of Agricultural Research at Tuskegee, Carver would spend the next few years experimenting with and developing hundreds of uses for peanuts, sweet potatoes, and soybeans. His scientific discoveries—including more than 300 products derived from peanuts, nearly 100 from sweet potatoes, about 75 from soybeans, and many more from Georgia clay—induced southern farmers to raise other crops in addition to cotton.

Success is not always something you strive for. It comes out of being obedient to what God tells you to do. Make sure your actions always line up with His directions, and you'll find success at every turn.

*Those who have trusted in God may be careful to devote themselves to doing what is good. These things are excellent and profitable for everyone.*

TITUS 3:8

GLDB

> *An investment in knowledge*
>
> *pays the best interest.*

In an episode of the TV series *The Andy Griffith Show*, the sheriff chastises a mischievous Ernest T. Bass, who has a penchant for throwing bricks and shattering windows. Reluctantly, Bass relents when he is threatened with jail time and then agrees not to throw any more bricks.

As the sheriff walks away, a devious-looking Bass reaches deep into his bag and pulls out a new weapon. Then, with a sheepish grin on his face, Bass says, "He didn't say nothing about no rock!"

It may have been that same attitude that led Clarence "Skip" Ellis, who grew up in a poor neighborhood on the south side of Chicago, to "bend the rules" a bit while working the graveyard shift at a local company to help support his family.

Ellis, whose job was mainly to prevent break-ins at the company, had been given specific instructions not to touch the company's brand-new computer. Obeying orders, the inquisitive fifteen-year-old used his free time on the job instead to read the manuals that came with the computer.

One day when the company had an urgent project but could not enter data into the computer because they had run out of new punch cards, Ellis came to the rescue. Through the knowledge he'd obtained from the manuals, Ellis was able to change some of the settings so that the used punch cards would work. The act saved the day and made Ellis an office hero. It also changed the direction of his life.

Ellis would go on to pursue his interest in computers and become the first African American to receive a Ph.D. in computer science.

When you are tempted to be disobedient, consider the times God has blessed you because you obeyed His Word. Then, trust God to help you continue to walk in obedience.

*God gave them knowledge and intelligence in every branch of literature and wisdom.*
DANIEL 1:17 NASB

A group of young men preparing to celebrate the birthday of Abraham Lincoln wanted James Johnson to speak at the occasion. His busy schedule not affording him the time to do so, Johnson instead wrote a poem and then asked his brother—a music teacher—to help him write a song from the poem.

Johnson recalled that while writing the words to "Lift Every Voice and Sing," the spirit of the poem took hold of him through two single lines near the end of the first stanza: "Sing a song full of the faith that the dark past has taught us. Sing a song full of the hope that the present has brought us."

> A good head and good heart are always a formidable combination.

A reflection on the fact that their strong faith in God is what helped his ancestors endure during the dark and bleak period of oppression and slavery, coupled with a hope for what the future might hold were Blacks ever to know true freedom, possibly inspired the next two lines: "Facing the rising sun of our new day begun, let us march on till victory is won."

Years later Johnson would reflect on the experience in his autobiography, telling how the song he and his brother, J. Rosamond Johnson, wrote was published and went on to become popular in churches, public schools, and civic organizations all over the South. So popular was it, in fact, that "Lift Every Voice and Sing" became known as "The Negro National Anthem," the victory cry of Black Americans.

When you follow your heart, you never know where you might end up. When you follow God, you always walk in the right direction. Let Him be your guide.

*My heart is steadfast, O God, my heart is steadfast;*
*I will sing and make music.*
PSALM 57:7

GLDB

## Anybody can start something.

There is an old saying that goes: "Good things come in small packages."

No one would expect for that small package to be a lunch box, but that turned out to be the case for Arthur George Gaston, the grandson of slaves who left behind a million-dollar empire when he died at age 103, despite never earning a high school diploma.

In the early 1920s, Gaston had moved his mother and grandmother from Birmingham to Westfield, Alabama, where he went to work in the coal mines. He quickly became disheartened to see that come payday, his coworkers found themselves left with little money after having borrowed against their pay from the "company store" to cover such things as food and rent.

Gaston knew there had to be a way to escape the trappings of a system that made it impossible for a man to get ahead. He found it in his lunchbox after realizing how attracted his coworkers were to its contents—

usually a tasty meal that included baked sweet potatoes, fried chicken, and biscuits.

Gaston had his mother, a former caterer, prepare extra food to sell to his coworkers. The boxed lunches would become Gaston's first business venture and the launching pad to a career that would see Gaston eventually rise to millionaire status.

Gaston died in 1996, leaving behind a fortune valued at well over $130 million and having built a business empire that included real estate, insurance, and communications.

You might see your talents and skills as small, but God can make something great from them. Take the little that you already have and ask God to build from it, so you can help others.

*Better is the end of a thing*
*than the beginning of it.*
ECCLESIASTES 7:8 AMP

Mae Jemison had been interested in outer space and space travel for as long as she could remember. Even when she was a youngster growing up in Chicago, the family would venture outside to watch the stars—without the aid of a telescope. Jemison also read books about space, hoping to learn as much as she could about the place she dreamed she would one day visit.

"I don't remember the time I said, 'I want to be an astronaut'; it's just always been there," Jemison would recall years after her dream came true.

In 1985, after years of study in related fields and earning a Bachelor of Science degree in chemical engineering from Stanford University and a Doctor of Medicine degree from Cornell University, Jemison began to actively pursue her dream of becoming an astronaut.

Though her first application for admission to the

*To struggle and battle and overcome and absolutely defeat every force designed against us is the only way to achieve.*

astronaut program at the National Aeronautics and Space Administration (NASA) was rejected, Jemison became 1 of only 15 candidates accepted out of 2,000 applicants the second time around in 1987. She successfully completed her astronaut training program in August 1988, becoming the fifth Black astronaut and the first Black female astronaut in NASA history.

When the space shuttle *Endeavor*, also known as *Spacelab J*, and its seven-member crew was launched into orbit on September 12, 1992, Mission Specialist Mae Jemison became the first Black woman astronaut to venture into space.

Things don't just happen. Sometimes, God orchestrates them and uses you to help them along. Be prepared.

*Faith that doesn't lead us to do good deeds is all alone and dead!*
JAMES 2:17 CEV

GLDB

## It's wiser being good than bad.

Recognized as the first Black superstar in the world of entertainment, singer Ethel Waters was an innovator who opened all the theatrical doors that up to her day had been closed to Black performers. But as Waters would later write in her autobiography, *His Eye Is on the Sparrow*, life for the successful Black singer did not start out so grand.

Born in 1896 to a twelve-year-old mother who had been raped by a white man, Waters was raised in poverty by her maternal grandmother. At age thirteen, she left school to work as a domestic to support herself.

Her singing career began with an amateur night performance in Philadelphia, then slowly moved through the Black theater circuit where she toured the South as "Sweet Mama Stringbean." When Waters introduced "Dinah" in 1925, she was signed to record for Columbia Records. She made her film debut in 1929, singing two songs in *On with the Show*. But a pivotal point came in 1933, when Waters' rendition of "Stormy Weather" made her the talk of the town.

Ironically, part of the song's lyrics reflected the storm that at times had raged in Waters' personal life:

*Life is bare, gloom and misery everywhere*

*Stormy weather, just can't get my poor old self together*

*I'm weary all the time, the time, so weary all of the time*

*All I do is pray, the Lord above will let me*

*Walk in the sun once more.*

In later years, after becoming a Christian, Waters abandoned the song.

"When I sang that song my life was like that," she once explained. "But it isn't anymore. Now my life is reflected in the songs I sing about God's love. If I get a heart attack, I'm not going to call on 'Stormy Weather,' I'm going to call on my Jesus."

Your life is reflected in everything you do and say. Make sure you are speaking words and singing songs that reflect God's goodness.

*[Jesus said,] "A good tree produces only good fruit, and a bad tree produces bad fruit. You can tell what a tree is like by the fruit it produces."*

MATTHEW 12:33 CEV

Ron was proud of the life he had made for himself and his family, even if it did mean being away from home for extended periods and during holidays. But the words spoken by a stranger he met in the airport terminal one day stopped him cold in his tracks.

"I never make plans that would cause me to be away from my family during holidays," the man said. "It's the one time of the year that families should always be together."

Silence filled the air as Ron nodded in agreement, but said nothing. Without intending, the man had spoken words that cut deep into his heart, bringing strong conviction.

Ron remembered a simpler time in his life, growing up in a poor Black family in the South. Times were hard, but holidays were special. The families he knew always spent them together.

*Where can a person be better than in the bosom of their family?*

Ron could smell the turkey roasting and the collard greens cooking. He could taste his mother's homemade sweet potato pie. And he could hear his father as he prayed over the meal, giving thanks to God for His bountiful provision and the blessing of family returning for the holidays.

Back then, being with family for the holiday was a tradition.

Today, at least in Ron's life, it had slipped away. Ron made a decision to make a change. "No more holidays away," he said aloud to himself.

How important is family to you?

Of all the things He values, family is one of God's most treasured creations. How high do your family relationships rank in your life?

*Behold, how good and how pleasant it is for brothers to dwell together in unity!*
PSALM 133:1 NASB

Next to our foreign policy no institution in American life is more hypocritical and therefore does more to hurt the cause of God and the cause of democracy than our so-called Christian church.

If the devil were to write his own beatitudes, they would probably read like this:

Blessed are those who are too tired, too busy, too distracted to spend an hour once a week with their fellow Christians in church. They are my best workers.

Blessed are those Christians who wait to be asked and expect to be thanked. I can use them.

Blessed are the touchy; with a bit of luck, they may stop going to church. They are my missionaries.

Blessed are those who are very religious but get on everyone's nerves. They are mine forever.

Blessed are the troublemakers. They shall be called my children.

Blessed are those who have no time to pray. They are easy prey for me.

Blessed are the gossipers. They are my secret agents.

Blessed are those critical of church leadership. They shall inherit a place with me in my fate.

Blessed are the complainers. I'm all ears for them.

Blessed are you when you read this and think it is about other people and not yourself.

I've got you!

The Word of God is like a road map. Follow it, and you will always reach the destination God has set for you. Get off track, and you will get lost. Choosing not to follow the direction given in the Bible is like volunteering your services to the devil. He welcomes you into his camp with open arms.

*You said to yourself, "I will ascend to heaven and set my throne above God's stars. ... I will climb to the highest heavens and be like the most High." But instead, you will be brought down to the place of the dead, down to its lowest depths.*
ISAIAH 14:13-15 NLT

As a white journalist researching the rise of suicide tendencies among southern Blacks, John Howard Griffin realized his research could never be accurate because "the southern Negro will not tell the white man the truth." To know what it was like to be Black and living in the South, Griffin had to experience it firsthand.

In 1959, Griffin used dyes, medication, and ultraviolet light to dramatically darken his skin. And for six weeks Griffin traveled across the Deep South—immersing himself in Black society and experiencing the racism and insults Blacks endured solely because of their skin color.

*Life is the only real counselor; wisdom unfiltered through personal experience does not become a part of the moral tissue.*

The transformation, Griffin would later write in the book *Black Like Me*, was shocking. "I had expected to see myself disguised, but this was something else. I was imprisoned in the flesh of an utter stranger, an unsympathetic one with whom I felt no kinship."

His experiences under the guise of a Black man would prove to be even more shocking. Like when he politely asked a white clerk for schedule information at a New Orleans bus station.

"She answered rudely and glared at me with such loathing I knew I was receiving what the Negroes call 'the hate stare,'" Griffin recalled. Another time, a white bus driver prevented the Blacks from getting off the bus during a rest stop in Mississippi.

"I sat in the monochrome gloom of dusk, scarcely believing that in this year of freedom any man could deprive another of anything so basic as the need to quench thirst or use the rest room," Griffin wrote.

Griffin's book helped to open the nation's eyes to the ills of racism.

Before you judge others, consider how you would feel if you were sitting where they are. Almighty God created you, created all mankind. His love for them should be a signal to you to show the same love.

*Remember those in prison as if you were their fellow prisoners, and those who are mistreated as if you yourselves were suffering.*

HEBREWS 13:3

> I am inclined to believe that a man may be free to do anything he pleases if only he will accept responsibility for whatever he does.

Joe Clark was no stranger to controversy when he signed on as director of the Essex County Detention House, a juvenile detention center in Newark, New Jersey, in August 1995. Some twelve years before, Clark had already made a name for himself in his home state as the "no-nonsense, drill sergeant" principal who knew what it took to bring order out of chaos at Eastside High School in Paterson, New Jersey.

In his seven years as principal, Clark held his students to high expectations, challenging them to succeed and confronting them when they failed. On a single day during his first week at Eastside, Clark, whose unusual means of communication included the use of a bullhorn, expelled three hundred students for fighting, vandalism, drug possession, profanity, and abusing teachers. Though it was never used as a weapon, Clark also wielded a baseball bat.

"If there is no discipline, there is anarchy," Clark

reasoned. "Good citizenship demands attention to responsibilities as well as rights."

Two years after Clark became principal, Eastside High was named a model school by New Jersey's governor. Although his methods were not universally accepted, Clark won national acclaim for his accomplishments. In addition to being named one of the nation's ten "Principals of Leadership" in 1986, Clark was the subject of a *Time* magazine cover story, featured twice on TV's *60 Minutes,* and appeared on several television news and talk shows. President Ronald Reagan named Clark a model educator and offered him a position as policy advisor, which Clark turned down.

Clark's story also became the subject of a 1989 movie called *Lean on Me.*

We sometimes shudder at the thought of having to discipline others when they have done wrong. But when God's love is applied, the correction will always go smoothly. Even the most difficult people will become peaceable.

*A youngster's heart is filled with foolishness,*
*but discipline will drive it away.*
PROVERBS 22:15 NLT

On July 25, 1916, an explosion at the Cleveland Waterworks in Ohio ripped through an underground tunnel 250 feet beneath Lake Erie, trapping 32 underground workers and killing 11 others. The deadly gases and heavy smoke that filled the underground spaces made rescue efforts difficult. In fact, 10 rescuers died trying.

Desperate for help, local police called on local business-man Garrett Morgan. Four years earlier, Morgan had designed a crude-looking breathing apparatus for use in smoke-filled atmospheres. The device consisted of a canvas hood that fit over the head. A double tube extending from the hood merged into a single tube at the back, the open end of which held a sponge soaked with water to filter out smoke and cool incoming air.

*Hope is the expectation that something outside of ourselves, something or someone external, is going to come to our rescue and we will live happily ever after.*

In a dramatic and heroic rescue effort, Morgan, his brother Frank, and two others used the device to successfully rescue the trapped workers and retrieve the bodies of the dead. The incident received national attention, and in the days that followed, fire departments around the country were calling Morgan's company to order the mask.

The Morgan gas mask was later refined for use by the U.S. Army, and during World War I it was used to protect soldiers from chlorine fumes. The mask was just one of several inventions credited to the extraordinary Black inventor and businessman.

One of Morgan's other successes was a traffic signal, patented in 1923. It featured a T-shaped pole unit with three positions: stop, go, and an "all-directional" stop position that halted traffic in all directions to allow pedestrians to cross streets safely.

The little we do now may not seem like much, but it could be part of God's plan for something greater. Stay open to ideas as though they are from God. Chances are they will be.

*In his heart a man plans his course,*
*but the LORD determines his steps.*
PROVERBS 16:9

GLDB

> *Helping others is*
> *like helping yourself.*

As a student at McGill University in Montreal, Canada, Charles Drew witnessed a man's life being saved by a blood transfusion. The experience had such an impact on him that he eventually devoted his life to the study of blood and blood plasma preservation.

The four different types of blood—A, B, AB, and O—had recently been discovered, so doctors could now determine what type of blood they were giving to patients. This alleviated the negative effects of mixing incompatible blood types. However, because whole blood was highly perishable and could only be stored for seven days, the problem of having the appropriate blood type readily available still existed.

Drew began to study the use of plasma as a substitute for whole blood. He found that because red blood cells contain the substance that determines blood type, their absence in plasma meant that a match between donor and recipient was not necessary.

Subsequently, Drew developed a method to process and preserve blood plasma so that it could be stored for long periods and shipped great distances.

His new method was first used in Europe and the Pacific where, at the height of World War II, there was a desperate shortage of blood to treat the wounded. It was during that time that Drew initiated the use of bloodmobiles—trucks equipped with refrigerators to store plasma.

Later, Drew organized the world's first blood-bank project and eventually established the American Red Cross Blood Bank. In 1940, he graduated from Columbia University and became the first African American to receive a Doctor of Science degree. Three years later, Drew became the first Black surgeon to serve as an examiner on the American Board of Surgery.

When you are convinced there is a better way, there usually is one. Trust God to show you.

*I [the Lord] will instruct you and teach you*
*in the way you should go; I will counsel you with*
*My eye upon you.*
PSALM 32:8 AMP

A self-educated scientist, inventor, and astronomer, Benjamin Banneker, became well known for his inventions and for writing a series of farmers' almanacs on such topics as medicine and astronomy. In 1753, he built a wooden pocket watch—the first watch made in America. Twenty years later, Banneker's calculations resulted in his successful forecast of a 1789 solar eclipse.

But as the descendent of slaves, Banneker was also an ardent supporter of his race and actively campaigned against slavery. In 1791, he sent a copy of his first almanac to then Secretary of State Thomas Jefferson. He included a letter questioning the slaveholder's sincerity as a "friend to liberty" and urging Jefferson to help get rid of the "absurd and false ideas" that one race is superior to another.

*It is never too late to give up our prejudices.*

Jefferson, who later became president of the United States, responded, in part:

Sir, I thank you sincerely for your letter and for the

Almanac it contained. No body wishes more than I do to see such proofs as you exhibit, that nature has given to our Black brethren talents equal to those of the other colors of men and that the appearance of a want of them is owing merely to the degraded condition of their existence, both in Africa and America. I can add with truth that nobody wishes more ardently to see a good system commenced for raising the condition both of their body and mind to what it ought to be, as fast as the imbecility of their present existence, and other circumstance which cannot be neglected, will admit … I am with great esteem, Sir, your most obedient, humble servant. Th. Jefferson.

Recognizing wrong is one thing; getting someone else to see it is another. Be thankful that God lets you see when you are wrong, and be quick to set things right. Ask Him for help when it comes to making others aware of their transgressions.

*If you have sinned, you should tell each other*
*what you have done. Then you can pray*
*for one another and be healed.*
JAMES 5:16 CEV

GLDB

*When your desires are strong enough,*

*you will appear to possess*

*superhuman powers to achieve.*

Patricia Bath never had problems with her eyesight that could not be fixed by the use of corrective lenses. But it bothered her that others, many of whom were suffering from blindness, had little hope of ever seeing again.

Believing that the limitations of science do not limit a person's imagination and that everyone has a "right to sight," Bath was convinced there was a way to treat patients who were either already blind or threatened with blindness because of cataracts. Her suspicions were confirmed through experiments she conducted using lasers.

In 1988, Bath became the first African-American woman doctor to receive a patent for a medical invention after designing the Cataract Laserphaco Probe, a laser device used to quickly and painlessly vaporize cataracts from patients' eyes. The method, which replaced the more common procedure of using a grinding, drill-like device to remove cataracts, transformed eye surgery. Not only did it increase the accuracy of cataract removal, but it also reduced the discomfort of the procedure.

Ultimately, Bath's invention was used to help restore sight to people who had been blind for more than thirty years.

By 1975, Bath, who had remained dedicated to the treatment and prevention of blindness, had attained a couple more "firsts." She became the first African-American woman surgeon at the UCLA Medical Center and the first woman to be on the faculty of the UCLA Jules Stein Eye Institute.

Compassion is God's way of telling you to reach out to others. Pay attention when you feel a sudden urge to help someone. You never know what the impact will be.

*As occasion and opportunity open up to us,*
*let us do good [morally] to all people [not only*
*being useful or profitable to them, but also doing*
*what is for their spiritual good and advantage].*
*Be mindful to be a blessing.*
GALATIANS 6:10 AMP

In her book *On Her Own Ground: The Life and Times of Madam C. J. Walker*, author Áelia Bundles describes her great-great grandmother as an early advocate of women's economic independence, a philanthropist who reconfigured the philosophy of charitable giving in the Black community, and a woman who "paved the way for profound social changes that altered the place of women in American society."

It is a description far from befitting a woman born in poverty. Sarah Breedlove—later known as Madam C. J. Walker—was the daughter of former slaves and orphaned at age seven. She worked in the cotton fields and was married by the time she was fourteen. But growing up in rural Louisiana, Sarah never saw herself as doomed to a life of poverty. Instead, she used her strong faith in God and determination to rise above her circumstances and reach out for success.

> *Always bear in mind that your own resolution to succeed is more important than any one thing.*

That success would come a few years later, when Sarah suddenly developed a scalp ailment that caused some hair loss. Sarah began experimenting with home remedies and products made by Black entrepreneur Annie Malone to correct the problem. In 1905, Sarah went to work for Malone and moved to Denver where she met and married St. Louis newspaperman, Charles Joseph Walker, her third husband.

Her business savvy soon proved profitable. She founded her own business and began selling a scalp conditioning and healing formula called Madam Walker's Wonderful Hair Grower. Before long the thriving national corporation employed more than three thousand people and included a broad offering of cosmetics, licensed agents, and schools.

Walker's faith, ambition, and drive resulted in a lofty accomplishment—the first known African-American woman to become a self-made millionaire.

Don't look at what you are. It could discourage you from ever becoming who God created you to be.

*Faith is being sure of what we hope for and certain of what we do not see.*
HEBREWS 11:1

*If you want to get somewhere, you have to know where you want to go and how to get there. Then never, never, never give up.*

Daniel's mother knew her hands would be full when she decided to convert a shed in the backyard of her home in Pensacola, Florida, into a makeshift classroom where she could teach her seventeen children and others from the neighborhood. But it was a small price for the schoolteacher to pay to ensure the youngsters would be prepared when it came time to confront the racial prejudices that awaited them in society.

She taught the children to strive for academic excellence, demonstrating that African Americans are inferior to none. If Blacks performed well, she told them, whites would acknowledge their achievements and racial discrimination would gradually end. Hence, the establishment of her "Eleventh Commandment": "Thou shalt never quit."

Though the problems of racism may have diminished, they have never fully come to an end. But as for maintaining a "never quit" attitude, Daniel found it to be sound advice.

While attending Tuskegee Institute in Florida, he joined the segregated United States Army Air Corps and pursued a career as an Air Force pilot. Although he missed seeing action during World War II, Daniel "Chappie" James eventually flew one hundred combat missions in Korea and Vietnam. By 1965, he had become a full colonel in the Air Force.

In 1967, he was named commander of Wheelus AFB in Libya just as Libya's leader, Colonel Moammar Khadafy, succeeded in his revolution there. A year later, James received his first star.

After four years in the Pentagon working in Public Affairs, where he earned two more stars, James was named vice commander of Military Airlift Command (MAC). Two years later, he made history by becoming the first African-American four-star general in the history of the military.

Perseverance in what you aspire to do is one way of achieving success. Recognizing that you need God's help in getting there and trusting Him to guide you is a guarantee that you will make it.

*I've got my eye on the goal, where God is beckoning us onward—to Jesus. I'm off and running, and I'm not turning back. So let's keep focused on that goal, those of us who want everything God has for us.*

PHILIPPIANS 3:13-15 MSG

Members of the Union Baptist Church in a South Philadelphia suburb held a benefit concert to raise money so one of their young members could take private singing lessons. The advertisements for the concert included a picture of the young girl and the words: "Come and hear the baby contralto, ten years old."

Nine years later, the young girl would find herself competing with three hundred others for a chance to perform with the New York Philharmonic Orchestra.

Marian Anderson won the competition and did, in fact, get a chance to sing with the famed orchestra. She went on to perform in England and Germany, where she received rave reviews for all 116 performances. But in 1939, Anderson planned a concert at the Constitution Hall in Washington, D.C., and members of the Daughters of the American Revolution (DAR), the group that owned the hall, refused to allow her to perform because she was Black.

The action was met with anger and outrage by

*Can one preach at home inequality of races and nations and advocate abroad good-will toward all men?*

Eleanor Roosevelt, who promptly resigned her DAR membership. The first lady then helped to arrange for Anderson to give an outdoor concert at the Lincoln Memorial. The event, held on Easter Sunday, drew more than seventy-five thousand people, who listened as Anderson opened by singing "America." Considered one of the most famous concerts ever given in the United States, it helped to open doors of opportunity for other African Americans.

Anderson went on to achieve several accomplishments. In Philadelphia, she became the first African American to receive the Bok Award, given to the citizen of whom the city is most proud. The $10,000 award was used to establish the Marian Anderson Scholarship Fund for music students of all races. Her historic debut with the Metropolitan Opera Company in January, 1955, marked the first time a Black singer had ever sung at the Metropolitan Opera.

There are several ways to get around obstacles. Trusting God for His help is the only sure way.

*Let every valley be lifted up, and every mountain and hill be made low; and let the rough ground become a plain, and the rugged terrain a broad valley.*

Isaiah 40:4 NASB

GLDB

> Hatred is gained as much by
> good works as by evil.

When he retired from major league baseball, Hank Aaron had racked up an impressive list of career records he could be proud of. Not only had the man who came to be known as "Hammerin' Hank" surpassed Babe Ruth's record to become the all-time leader with 755 home runs, Aaron also set 12 other records, including most home runs with one club (Braves, 733); most RBIs (2,297); total bases (6,856); and most games played (3,298).

In addition, Aaron, who was named to the Baseball Hall of Fame in 1982, after hitting 20 or more home runs for 20 consecutive seasons, was named to 24 all-star games and won 3 Gold Glove awards. But by the time his career ended, there would be one other record the famed slugger would garner—one he was not particularly proud of.

For a period in 1973, as he closed in on Ruth's home-run record, Aaron received an estimated three thousand pieces of racist hate mail each day—more letters than any American outside of politics. Though obviously disturbed that so many people could be against him, Aaron did not let the hatred distract him from his goal. On April 8, 1974, the largest crowd in Braves' history—53,775 fans—came out to witness history in the making.

Aaron would later reflect on the letters he received, saying: "I read the letters because they remind me not to be surprised or hurt. They remind me of what people are really like." After retiring, Aaron became one of the first Blacks in major league baseball's upper management, serving as vice president of player development for the Atlanta Braves.

God's Word is always true. It is only when you close your eyes to the truth that you position yourself to be deceived. Facing the truth is always the best way—God's way—to do anything.

*Jesus said, "If you hold to my teaching, you are really my disciples. Then you will know the truth, and the truth will set you free."*

JOHN 8:31-32

Growing up in White Plains, Virginia, Malvin Russell Goode could have adopted the philosophy of his father who, with only a third-grade education, thought it more advantageous to work than to strive for an education. Instead, the youngster held fast to the encouragement of his mother, who stressed the importance of an education and always told her children: "You are no better than anyone else and no one is better than you. Now go out and prove it."

Prove it is just what Goode did.

In the early 1960s, the journalist was working on the staff of the *Pittsburgh Courier* when he received a call from ABC television in New York City, asking that he interview for a job as a reporter. After reading a script he had prepared for the interview, Goode was offered the job and became the first African-American news reporter for a major network.

One month later, the country woke up on a Sunday morning to the news of the Cuban missile crisis and the

> *Shortchange your education now and you may be short of change the rest of your life.*

voice and face of correspondent Mal Goode.

"I went on at twenty-five minutes after ten when they broke into the [regularly scheduled] program," Goode later recalled. "This was the first time my family had seen me on TV, and they started calling from across the country."

Ultimately, Goode conducted interviews with famous and influential people like civil rights leader Martin Luther King Jr.; boxer Muhammad Ali; former President George Bush Sr.; and baseball great Jackie Robinson, another African American who broke a racial barrier when he became the first African American to play in the major leagues.

God gives you plenty of opportunities to do something good—either for yourself or someone else. Make sure you recognize His knock and answer with a ready heart and mind.

*Observe people who are good at their work—
skilled workers are always in demand and
admired; they don't take a back seat to anyone.*
PROVERBS 22:29 MSG

GLDB

## It is hard for an empty bag to stand upright.

Outspoken on the issues of human rights and racial injustice, abolitionist Frederick Douglass often tried to encourage Blacks that they could be somebody. He once shared this story:

"I once knew a little colored boy whose mother and father died when he was but six years old," Douglass began. "He was a slave and had no one to care for him. He slept on a dirt floor in a hovel and in cold weather would crawl into a meal bag, head foremost, and leave his feet in the ashes to keep them warm.

"Often he would roast an ear of corn and eat it to satisfy his hunger, and many times he crawled under the barn or stable and secured eggs, which he would roast in the fire and eat. That boy did not wear pants like you and I do, but a tow linen shirt.

"Schools were unknown to him, and he learned to spell from an old Webster's spelling book and read and write from posters on cellar doors. He would then preach and speak and soon became well known. He became a United States elector, United States marshal, United States recorder, United States diplomat, and accumulated some wealth. He wore broadcloth and didn't have to divide crumbs with the dogs under the table.

"That boy was Frederick Douglass.

"What was possible for me is possible for you," Douglass told the students. "Don't think because you are colored you can't accomplish anything. Strive earnestly to add to your knowledge. So long as you remain in ignorance, so long will you fail to command the respect of your fellowmen."

God's Spirit will give you wisdom, knowledge, and understanding so that you can skillfully handle situations and solve problems. Just ask Him and believe He will answer you.

*"My people are destroyed from lack of knowledge."*
HOSEA 4:6

Being equal can sometimes still mean you are separate. Ada Lois Sipuel discovered this through her apparent victory as the first African-American woman to attend an all-white law school in the South.

Born in Chickasha, Oklahoma, Sipuel took a bold step in 1946 when she decided to challenge the segregationist policies of the University of Oklahoma School of Law, after being denied entry because of her race. A younger brother had initially planned to make the challenge. He enrolled at Howard University School of Law instead because he did not want to delay his career due to litigation.

*The important thing is this: to be able at any moment to sacrifice what we are for what we could become.*

In 1948, the Supreme Court ruled that the state of Oklahoma must provide instruction for Blacks equal to that of whites. When she was finally admitted to the OU law school, Ada, who was by then married and expecting her first child, was given a special seat marked "colored" that was roped off from the rest of the class. She was also forced to eat in a separate chained-off, guarded area of the law school cafeteria.

Years later, Ada Sipuel Fisher would recall how supportive some of her classmates and teachers were, often sharing their notes to help her catch up in her studies and sometimes crossing the chained-off area to have lunch with her. Fisher said it was necessary for her to endure the negative treatment because "I knew the eyes of Oklahoma and the nation were on me."

In 1951, Fisher graduated with a master's degree. A year later she began practicing law in her hometown of Chickasha. When she was appointed to the Board of Regents of the University of Oklahoma in 1992, Fisher acknowledged it as the culmination of a forty-five-year cycle in her life.

God can turn your trials into triumphs and then use them as a gateway for others to succeed.

*He was beaten, he was tortured, but he didn't say a word. Like a lamb taken to be slaughtered and like a sheep sheared, he took it all in silence.*

ISAIAH 53:7 MSG

GLDB

## Never let the other fellow set the agenda.

Tradition has it that in 1903, in Rockdale, Texas, a stubborn Texas Longhorn steer refused to enter a corral. The animal raised such a ruckus that it kept scattering the herd.

Having had enough of the ornery critter, a young cowhand by the name of Bill decided to take matters into his own hands. Riding his horse at high speed alongside the cantankerous, rampaging longhorn, the cowboy jumped off his steed onto the back of the steer, grabbed him by the horns, and wrestled him to the ground. When the animal continued to resist, the cowboy bit it on its lower lip and slammed it to the ground.

The incident lead to the introduction of a new regular attraction on the rodeo circuit called "bulldogging" or "steer-wrestling," and Bill Pickett, the young ranch hand who introduced it, went on to become the most famous Black rodeo performer ever. In

1971, Pickett, who descended from American Indian and Black slave stock and grew up in West Texas, became the first African-American cowboy to be inducted into the Rodeo Hall of Fame. A statue of Pickett wrestling a bovine can be seen on display at the Cowboy Coliseum in Fort Worth, Texas.

Pickett is also featured as one of the stars of the "Legends of the West" stamp series issued by the United States Postal Service.

You may never literally take a bull by the horns, but there will be times when bringing a matter under control will require a take-charge attitude. Ask God for the courage, strength, and wisdom to do His will in any situation.

*[Jesus said,] I am coming quickly; hold fast what you have, so that no one may rob you and deprive you of your crown.*
REVELATION 3:11 AMP

It had been a stressful workday for the forty-two-year-old Black seamstress when she mistakenly boarded a bus in Montgomery, Alabama, that was operated by a white driver named James Black. She well remembered the day some twelve years earlier when she was thrown off of Black's bus after refusing to pay at the front of the bus and then reboard at the rear.

Despite the fact that nearly two-thirds of the passengers who rode the city buses were Black, the buses were sectioned off so that ten seats up front were designated for whites and 10 seats in the rear were for the Black passengers. At his discretion, the driver determined who sat in the middle. If the bus was crowded, Blacks were expected to give up their seats to whites and stand in the aisle.

> I am not afraid of storms, for I have learned how to sail my ship.

On this particular day, however, a fatigued Rosa Parks chose a seat in the middle of the bus. As the bus became crowded, the driver ordered Parks to give up her seat to a white passenger. When Parks refused, she was arrested and later fined for violating a city ordinance. A young preacher named Martin Luther King Jr. heard about the incident and, with the cooperation of some seventeen thousand Black residents, launched a bus boycott in Montgomery that lasted for more than a year. In the end, the Supreme Court intervened and declared segregation on buses to be unconstitutional.

That single incident sparked a movement that would eventually lead to an end to segregation in America and Parks coming to be known as "the mother of the Civil Rights Movement."

Standing up for what is right may not be easy for you or others. But the satisfaction comes in knowing you have pleased the Master and that good will surely follow.

*Put on all the armor that God gives. Then … you will be able to defend yourself. And when the battle is over, you will still be standing firm.*

EPHESIANS 6:13 CEV

> The bravest sight in all the world is a
> man fighting against odds.

As the deep, menacing voice of Darth Vader in the *Star Wars* films, actor James Earl Jones had no problems articulating his purpose to destroy the Jedi knights. But in reality, the character was a far cry from that of the quiet, reserved boy from Arkabutla Township, Mississippi, who suffered from a stuttering problem as a child.

The product of a broken home, Jones spent much of his early years in near silence, refusing to speak more than a few words at a time—even to his family. In school, he pretended to be mute and communicated only in writing.

Jones would eventually overcome his insecurities with the help of a high school teacher. For a class project, Jones wrote a poem that impressed the teacher. Pretending not to believe Jones had composed the poem, the teacher challenged him to read it out loud before the class. Jones responded by reciting the poem from memory—without stuttering.

Eventually, Jones took up acting as a way to combat the affliction, earning a bachelor's degree in drama. He is perhaps best known for his leading roles in Shakespeare's *Othello* and in *The Great White Hope*, a play about the tragic career of Jack Johnson, the first Black heavyweight-boxing champion.

The turning point in Jones' acting career came with the role of Vader. While younger audiences may not know the man, they recognize the voice as that of King Mufasa in the animated classic *The Lion King*. Jones is also heard by millions of news watchers around the world every day through the words, "This is CNN."

A handicap can be a permanent hindrance, if you allow it to be. Given to God, however, it can transform you and the world around you.

*[Jesus said,] "Have peace in me. Here on earth you will have many trials and sorrows. But take heart, because I have overcome the world."*

JOHN 16:33 NLT

When television newswoman Barbara Walters' TV special "The Ten Most Fascinating People of 1995" aired years ago, most everyone watching was familiar with nine of the ten people being honored. The list included tennis star Monica Seles, John F. Kennedy Jr., Jim Carey, Dr. Rick Nelson, Ted Turner, Newt Gingrich, Christopher Reeve, Courtney Love, and former Secretary of State Colin Powell.

But unless they knew her personally, the name Oseola McCarty, the tenth honoree, might not have registered.

*Self-sacrifice is the real miracle out of which all the reported miracles grow.*

Before she gained fame by donating $150,000 to the University of Southern Mississippi in 1995, McCarty had lived in virtual obscurity, spending the last seventy-five years washing and ironing clothes for generations of families in her modest home. That's how she saved so much money.

From the beginning, McCarty charged $1.50 to $2 to do a bundle of laundry. With inflation, the price eventually rose to $10. But as a single woman who rarely left home except to do grocery shopping, McCarty had little use for money.

"Sometime after the war, I commenced to save money," she recalled during an interview. "I put it into savings. I never would take any of it out. I just put it in. It just accumulated."

McCarty, who left school after the sixth grade to care for an ailing relative, says she gave the money because, "I wanted to help somebody's child go to college." Her gift endowed the Oseola McCarty Scholarship for African-American students who demonstrate financial need. Hers became the largest gift ever given to the school by an African American.

Giving is one of the best ways to show you care, especially when you don't look for something in return. God's love for you was shown when He asked His Son to give His life for you. The greatest gift you can give Him in return is your life—the one He gave so much to redeem.

*He who is generous will be blessed,*
*for he gives some of his food to the poor.*
PROVERBS 22:9 NASB

GLDB

> What an enormous magnifier is tradition!
> How a thing grows in the human memory
> and in the human imagination when love,
> worship, and all that lies in the human
> heart, is there to encourage it.

Not many people would be up for traveling overseas by the time they're pushing ninety years of age. But if the mission was one of goodwill, that would be another story.

George H. Black, a well-known African-American brick maker, was on such a mission in 1970 when, at the spry old age of ninety-one, he left his home in Winston-Salem, North Carolina, and traveled to Guyana to share his age-old craft with the villages of that country. The commission, which garnered Black national news attention, was at the request of the state government.

The son of a former slave, Black moved to Winston-Salem as a boy and hauled bricks for a white brick maker. Soon after, Black started his own brick-yard and established a national and international reputation for producing bricks of quality and durability. As early as the 1920s, Black's work was sought after for its traditional eighteenth- and nineteenth-century craftsmanship and techniques.

Recognized as "the last brick maker in America," Black made an exceptionally important contribution to the twentieth century by sustaining traditional handcrafting of bricks when most brick makers had abandoned this practice for more efficient brick-making machines. In the 1940s, Black established a brickyard approximately one hundred feet behind his residence, which he continued to operate until the 1970s. The George Black House and Brickyard, where Black lived and worked until his death in 1980 at age 101, is now part of the National Register of Historic Places.

It's not always necessary to reinvent the wheel, especially when doing things the "old-fashioned way" works just as well. God never changes, and His ways are perfect. God will let you know when some aspect of your life needs change—and He will show you how to go about it.

*Every good and perfect gift comes down from the Father who created all the lights in the heavens. He is always the same and never makes dark shadows by changing.*
JAMES 1:17 CEV

Speaking to a group of professional secretaries, civil rights attorney Ruby Grant Martin once shared some encouraging words from her father that set the course for her life:

"While my father instilled me with pride, enthusiasm, and self confidence, perhaps the most important thing he did for me was to tell me that I was smart, that I could be anything I wanted to be, and that I have to be something important," Martin said. "He said that because I was so smart and competent that I had a special gift and that gift carried with it a special responsibility—that responsibility was to make a difference and to leave a legacy of achievements and successes so that people would know that I had been here."

> I expect to pass through this life but once. Therefore, if there be any kindness I can show, or any good thing I can do for another human being, let me do it now, for I shall not pass this way again.

Throughout her career as a federal and state attorney and as an administrator, Martin sought to live up to those words and make a difference as an advocate for the improvement of economic and educational opportunities for Blacks. Many of her efforts were directed toward assuring legal protection for minorities and the poor and helping to affect better lives for women and children.

In 1967, she became the first director of the Office for Civil Rights in the U.S. Department of Health, Education, and Welfare. She was in charge of a federal school desegregation program, entrusted with the task of facilitating employment and affirmative action programs of the Civil Rights Act of 1964. Martin had also served as the Virginia secretary of administration under Governor L. Douglas Wilder.

Martin received numerous awards for her service, including the NAACP's Freedom Fund Award in 1991.

Taking what you have and using it to make life better for others is one of the greatest forms of service. Even if what you have seems small and insignificant to you, God can use it to do great things. What do you have that you can share?

*Whoever heard me spoke well of me, and those who saw me commended me, because I rescued the poor who cried for help, and the fatherless who had none to assist him.*

JOB 29:11-12

GLDB

> Let me be a little kinder,
>
> Let me be a little blinder
>
> To the faults of those around me.

A little boy entered a coffee shop one day and took a seat at a table. Within seconds, the waitress approached and put a glass of water down in front of him.

"How much is an ice cream sundae?" the young boy asked.

"Fifty cents," replied the waitress.

The little boy pulled his hand out of his pocket and carefully studied a number of coins he held. Then, he looked up at the waitress.

"How much is a dish of plain ice cream?" he inquired.

By then, other customers were coming in and waiting for a table. The waitress was growing visibly impatient with the youngster.

"Thirty-five cents," she responded irritably.

The little boy again counted the coins, then made

his decision.

"I'll have the plain ice cream," he told the waitress.

The waitress brought the ice cream, set it down in front of the boy, and walked away. When the boy had finished his treat, he paid the cashier and left. Moments later, the waitress returned to the table to prepare it for the next customer.

Shocked and surprised, the waitress swallowed hard at what she saw on the table. There, placed neatly beside the empty ice cream dish, were two nickels and five pennies. It was her tip!

Kindness is sometimes rewarded even when it is not due. Always follow the golden rule, and do for others just as you would have them do for you. God does not forget the kindness you show to others. He is always faithful to return it to you.

*Be kind to one another, tenderhearted, forgiving one another, even as God in Christ forgave you.*
Ephesians 4:32 NKJV

Beginning today, I will …

- no longer worry about yesterday. It is in the past and the past will never change. Only I can change by choosing to do so.

- no longer worry about tomorrow. Tomorrow will always be there, waiting for me to make the most of it. But I cannot make the most of tomorrow without first making the most of today.

*To each day its own resources.*

- look in the mirror, and I will see a person worthy of my respect and admiration. This capable person looking back at me is someone I enjoy spending time with and someone I would like to get to know better.

- cherish each moment of my life. I value this gift bestowed upon me in this world, and I will unselfishly share this gift with others.

- take life one day at a time, one step at a time. Discouragement will not be allowed to taint my positive self-image, my desire to succeed, or my capacity to love.

- walk with renewed faith in human kindness. Regardless of what has gone before, I believe there is hope for a brighter and better future.

- open my mind and my heart; welcome new experiences; meet new people. I will not expect perfection from myself or anyone else: perfection does not exist in an imperfect world. But I will applaud the attempt to overcome human foibles.

- learn something new; I will try something different; I will savor all the various flavors life has to offer. I will change what I can, and the rest I will let go. I will strive to become the best me I can possibly be.

Beginning today—and every day.

What changes can you make in your life, beginning today, that would make you a better Christian? God gives you several opportunities each day to show others His love. It is up to you to take advantage of them.

*This is good and pleases God our Savior.*
1 TIMOTHY 2:3 NLT

GLDB

> True heroism is remarkably sober, very undramatic. It is not the urge to surpass all others at whatever cost, but the urge to serve others at whatever cost.

The name Lawrence Joel is not one that is likely to be recognized by many people around the country. And that's probably how the former soldier and Army medic would have wanted it. But it is hard to keep him out of the spotlight after being cited for bravery and honored with the Congressional Medal of Honor, the first living Black American to have received the prestigious medal since the Spanish-American War in 1898.

Such an honor came to Specialist Six Lawrence Joel, a Winston-Salem, North Carolina, native, who was cited for gallantry and intrepidity at the risk of his life above and beyond the call of duty. Joel earned the medal for his heroic actions that took place on November 8, 1965, while serving as a medical corpsman in Vietnam.

During an intense attack, Joel left his cover to administer aid to several of his fallen comrades, giving them plasma, pain killers, and other medication.

A commendation issued by the government stated

that Joel "demonstrated indomitable courage, determination, and professional skill. After treating the men wounded by the initial burst of gunfire, he bravely moved forward to assist others who were wounded. Although painfully wounded, his desire to aid his fellow soldiers transcended all personal feeling. He bandaged his own wound and self-administered morphine to deaden the pain, enabling him to continue his dangerous undertaking.

"Throughout the long battle, Joel never lost sight of his mission as a medical aidman and continued to comfort and treat the wounded until his own evacuation was ordered. His meticulous attention to duty saved a large number of lives, and his unselfish, daring example under most adverse conditions was an inspiration to all."

When you have true love for others, you'll do whatever it takes to guard their safety—even if it means putting your life on the line. Self-sacrifice is the ultimate testimony of God's love abiding deep within your heart.

*For a good man someone might possibly dare to die. But God demonstrates his own love for us in this: While we were still sinners, Christ died for us.*

ROMANS 5:7-8

Growing up in Philadelphia, TV journalist Ed Bradley never allowed himself to be swept up in goals. Instead, Bradley once recalled in an interview, "I have standards of achievement.

"I was raised by people who worked twenty-hour days at two jobs each. I was told, 'You can be anything you want, kid.' When you hear that often enough, you believe it."

Believing he could be anything he wanted was all the motivation a young Bradley needed to strike out on a path that would eventually lead to his becoming one of the top TV news correspondents in the country.

It's good to have people supporting your dreams and cheering you on to the winner's circle. But what do you do when there is no cheering squad? Or when no one around you appears to be as confident of your abilities as you are?

Setting goals is one thing. How you go about

*The best thing about the future is that it comes only one day at a time.*

achieving them makes all the difference in the world. In fact, when it comes to success or failure, your actions are key.

In the Bible, God encourages us to set goals. But He also stresses the importance of staying focused on whatever plans you have for the future. In Habakkuk 2:2, He tells us to write down the vision. Then keep an eye on it so it won't slip away.

Not everyone grows up to be what he or she wants to be. But if you allow Him, God will grow you up to be what He wants you to be. And you won't be disappointed. Trust Him. He knows what's best for you.

*Be strong and do not give up,*
*for your work will be rewarded.*
2 Chronicles 15:7

> Great things are not done by impulse,
> but by a series of small things
> brought together.

His friends call him *Q* for short. But the single letter could just as easily stand for *quality*, which is only one way to describe his musical genius. But it wasn't always that way for the youngster who was born Quincy Delight Jones Jr.

A product of Chicago's gang-ridden South Side, Jones found life to be a challenge during his early years.

"Our biggest struggle every day was we were either running from gangs or with gangs," Jones once recalled.

When he was ten, Jones got away from the dangers of the streets when he moved with his family to Bremerton, Washington. There, while still in elementary school, he began what would eventually become a love relationship with music, trying his hand at nearly every instrument before settling on the trumpet.

Music became a passion for Jones. And in the years that followed, that passion served as an escape from the dangers that surrounded him and a door to becoming one of the most successful African-American music producers in history. The quality of his music resulted in a number of achievements, including his becoming the all-time most Grammy-nominated artist with a total of seventy-six nominations and twenty-six awards.

What letter of the alphabet would best describe you?

Would the letter *F* show how *faithful* you are in your service to God. Maybe *P* would show how *patiently* you wait while He completes the good work He has begun in you. Or, perhaps people would describe you by the letter *T* because you have such a strong *trust* in the Lord.

Whatever your passion is in life, let it be fueled by patiently and faithfully trusting in God to help you fulfill it.

*Do you see a man diligent and skillful in his business? He will stand before kings.*
PROVERBS 22:29 AMP

While at the park one day, a woman sat down next to a man on a bench near a playground.

"That's my son over there," she said, pointing to a little boy in a red sweater who was gliding down the slide.

"He's a fine looking boy," the man said. "That's my son on the swing in the blue sweater."

Then, looking at his watch, the man called to his son.

"What do you say we go, Todd?"

"Just five more minutes, Dad," the young boy pleaded. "Just five more minutes."

> Truly appreciate life, and you'll find that you have more of it.

The man nodded in agreement, and his son continued to swing to his heart's content. Minutes passed, and the father stood and called again to his son.

"Time to go now," he said.

Again, the young boy pleaded: "Five more minutes, Dad, just five more minutes."

The man smiled and said OK.

Noticing the father's attitude toward his son, the woman said: "My, you certainly are a patient father."

The man smiled and then said, "My older son, Tommy, was killed by a drunk driver last year while he was riding his bike near here. I never spent much time with Tommy, and now I'd give anything for just five more minutes with him. I've vowed not to make the same mistake with Todd. He thinks he has five more minutes to swing. The truth is, I get five more minutes to watch him play."

Too often we take for granted the things that mean the most to us. Think of what you would have missed if God had not waited patiently for you to accept His invitation and come to Him. His love is never ending, and His patience is forever enduring. Let that be your example.

*There's nothing better for us ... than to have a good time in whatever we do—that's our lot. Who knows if there's anything else to life?*

ECCLESIASTES 3:22 MSG

GLDB

> Kindness can become its own motive.
> We are made kind by being kind.

There isn't much that I can do,
but I can share my bread with you,
and sometimes share a sorrow too.

There isn't much that I can do,
but I can sit an hour with you,
and I can share a joke or two,
and sometimes share reverses too.

There isn't much that I can do,
but I can share my flowers with you,
and I can share my books with you,
and sometimes share your burdens too.

There isn't much that I can do,
but I can share my hopes with you,
and I can share my fears with you,
and sometimes shed some tears with you.

There isn't much that I can do,
but I can share my friends with you,
and I can share my life with you,
and oftentimes share a prayer with you.

God gave the greatest gift of all when He gave His only Son, Christ Jesus, as a sacrifice for the sins of man. That includes you and me. He gave His best so that others might benefit. What "best" do you have that you are willing to give for the benefit of others?

*Do not be hardhearted or tightfisted toward your poor brother. Rather be openhanded and freely lend him whatever he needs.*
DEUTERONOMY 15:7-8

Long before entering the military, Sherian Grace Cadoria was getting a taste of the strict discipline she would eventually encounter. Her mother once made Cadoria and her siblings walk five miles back to a store to return an extra penny a cashier had mistakenly given in their change.

That may be small to some, but for Cadoria it represented the Christian integrity that had been instilled in her while growing up. It was the same integrity she would have to exude in her position as the first Black woman in the regular U.S. Army to achieve the rank of brigadier general.

*There is no teaching to compare with example.*

"I've gotten more pressure from being female in a man's world than from being Black," Cadoria once said. "I was always a role model. I had responsibility not just for Black women but for Black men as well. A woman today has to do more than her male counterpart. I came in knowing I was going to have to give 200 percent effort to get 100 percent credit."

Cadoria's journey began at Southern University in Baton Rouge, where she was selected by the Women's Army Corps to represent the school at the College Junior Program. She spent four weeks at Fort McClellen in the summer of 1960 and experienced firsthand the life of an enlisted soldier.

During a two-year stint in Vietnam, Cadoria often took on assignments not normally given to women. She garnered several "firsts," including being the first woman to command an all-male battalion; the first woman to lead a criminal-investigation brigade; and the first Black woman to be admitted to the elite army schools. Cadoria was promoted to brigadier general in 1985, making her the highest-ranking Black woman in the armed forces.

The greatest role model of all is God. When you pattern your words and actions after Him, you can achieve great things no matter what obstacles lie in your path—and you will become an amazing role model for others as well.

*Be an example (pattern) for the believers in speech, in conduct, in love, in faith, and in purity.*
1 TIimothy 4:12 AMP

GLDB

Coretta Scott was quite familiar with the injustices of life in a segregated society as a child growing up in Alabama. Raised on a farm with her parents, she walked five miles a day to attend the one-room schoolhouse while the white students rode buses to an all-white school closer by.

"I was told, one way or another, almost every day of my life, that I wasn't as good as a white child," Scott remembers. "Such messages, saying we were inferior, were a daily part of our lives."

But being raised in a godly home in Alabama, where her parents emphasized strong values of self-worth, Scott knew better than to let what others think determine the kind of person she would become.

> You are what you think. You are what you go for. You are what you do.

"I was blessed with parents who taught me not to let anyone make me feel like I wasn't good enough, and as my mother told me, 'You are just as good as anyone else. You get an education and try to be somebody. Then you won't have to be kicked around by anybody, and you won't have to depend on anyone for your livelihood, not even a man.'"

The words became a driving force for Scott, who took an active interest in the Civil Rights Movement during college. She joined the NAACP and served on race relations and civil liberties committees. Little did she know that her connection with civil rights would soon become even more involved as the wife of civil rights leader, Dr. Martin Luther King Jr., whom Scott met while studying concert singing at New England Conservatory of Music in Boston.

The couple married on June 18, 1953, and the following year moved to Montgomery, Alabama, where King became pastor of the Dexter Avenue Baptist Church. Coretta Scott King and her husband later found themselves caught up in the dramatic events that triggered the modern Civil Rights Movement.

When others try to define who you are, remember that God has given you His mark of excellence. He has a plan for your life, regardless of what others may say or do.

*I'm so grateful to Christ Jesus for making me adequate to do this work.*
1 TIMOTHY 1:12 MSG

GLDB

> Inferiority is what you enjoy
> in your best friends.

Former Secretary of State Colin Powell has often related the story of his returning home from Vietnam in 1963 and an incident that propelled him to want to change the way whites view Black people.

"I was busy trying to get a home ready for my family. I found a place in Phoenix City, Alabama, which was not a great place to live as a Black in those days.

"One night after working on the house, I tried to buy a hamburger at a drive-in place in Columbus. I knew I couldn't go in; I didn't try to go in. I just tried to order it on the little speaker box for it to be brought out. The young lady came out to take my order, the way it was done in those days, and she looked in the car and she asked me if I was Puerto Rican, and I said no.

"Then she asked me if I was an African student studying at the infantry school. I said, 'No, I'm not an African student studying at the infantry school; I'm an American.'

"'I'm terribly sorry,' she said, 'but I can't bring it out to the car. You'll have to get out and go around to the back.'

"'Thank you very much, no thanks,' I said, and I drove off."

Asked how the incident affected him, Powell called it "deeply hurtful and disappointing.

"If anything, it encouraged me, motivated me, caused me to find ways to demonstrate to people who held such beliefs that their beliefs had to be incorrect, had to be a lie," said Powell, who went on to became the first African American to hold the office of secretary of state.

While others may see you as inferior, God, the Almighty Father who created you in His image, sees you as His equal. You are His son or daughter, and He treats you with the same love and respect that He gives Jesus. When you consider that truth, the unenlightened views of others are hardly worth the time it takes to dismiss them.

*What marvelous love the Father has extended to us!*
*Just look at it—we're called children of God!*
*That's who we really are. But that's also why*
*the world doesn't recognize us.*
1 JOHN 3:1 MSG

When you thought I wasn't looking, I saw you hang my first painting on the refrigerator, and I immediately wanted to paint another one.

When you thought I wasn't looking, I saw you feed a stray cat, and I learned that it was good to be kind to animals.

When you thought I wasn't looking, I heard you say a prayer, and I knew there is a God I could always talk to, and I learned to trust in God.

When you thought I wasn't looking, I saw you make a meal and take it to a friend who was sick, and I learned that we all have to help take care of each other.

> *Example is not the main thing in influencing others. It is the only thing.*

When you thought I wasn't looking, I saw you give of your time and money to help people who had nothing, and I learned that those who have something should give to those who don't.

When you thought I wasn't looking, I saw you take care of our house and everyone in it, and I learned we have to take care of what we are given.

When you thought I wasn't looking, I saw tears come from your eyes, and I learned that sometimes things hurt, but it's all right to cry.

When you thought I wasn't looking, I saw that you cared, and I wanted to be everything that I could be.

When you thought I wasn't looking, I learned most of life's lessons from you that I need to know to be a good and productive person when I grow up.

When you thought I wasn't looking, I looked at you and wanted to say, "Thanks for all the things I saw when you thought I wasn't looking."

Others are watching you, especially those growing up in your home. And what they see is the legacy you will one day leave behind. Will they see that you trust and revere God? Will they see you turn to Him for help, comfort, and wisdom? Will they see you thank Him for all He does in your life?

*Jesus … said, "I am the light for the world! Follow me, and you won't be walking in the dark."*
JOHN 8:12 CEV

GLDB

> Every life is a profession of faith,
> and exercises an inevitable
> and silent influence.

Ossie Davis could look to several things in his early years that influenced his decisions both to become an actor and to champion the cause of Blacks against racial injustice. One that stands out, however, was a trip to Washington, D.C., in 1939, where Davis heard singer Marian Anderson performing at the Lincoln Memorial. Because of her color, Anderson had been barred from performing at Constitution Hall.

"I understood fully for the first time the importance of Black song, Black music, Black arts," Davis recalls. "I was handed my spiritual assignment that night."

Davis—whose real name was Raiford Chatman Davis—had a revelation early in life that inspired him. He saw himself not only as one destined for success, but as someone called to make a difference in the lives of others. In later years Davis did become a success in the field of acting. He and his wife, Ruby Dee, were among the first Black-American actors to break out of traditional "Negro" roles. They are credited as having opened many doors that had been previously closed to African-American artists.

Not everyone is called to stand out in a crowd as a leader. But every now and then God chooses one whose heart is right—one He knows He can trust to follow Him and not seek his own fame and fortune—and assigns him to a task meant to benefit others. What assignment has God handpicked for you? Whatever it is, be assured that as you follow, God will part the waters before you and equip you with every skill, every opportunity, every resource you need to accomplish all He's called you to do.

*Each of us is to please his neighbor*
*for his good, to his edification.*
ROMANS 15:2 NASB

As one of the biggest musical acts in history, the British rock group the Beatles dominated the music charts for most of the 1960s. Not a single group could touch them. But that was not to be the case in 1964, when, despite the fact that they had five straight number-one albums, Beatlemania was forced to give way to a single Broadway tune and the raspy voice of a Black trumpet player named Louis Armstrong.

That year, Armstrong's recording of "Hello Dolly" became the number-one song on the Billboard charts, replacing the Beatles' bouncy love song, "I Want to Hold Your Hand." That same year, Armstrong won a Grammy Award for "Hello Dolly." It was a year of redemption for a man who, as a poor child growing up in New Orleans, had such love and compassion that he sometimes spent his nights singing on street corners to make money to help support the family.

It would be that same type of compassion that

*To be free means the ability to deal with the realities of one's situation so as not to be overcome by them.*

followed Louis "Satchmo" Armstrong into adulthood where, as an unofficial international ambassador of jazz and swing, he would use his music to bring joy and happiness to many. With his infectious grin, his warm and friendly sense of humor, and his unassuming manner, Armstrong would go on to become one of the most recognized and popular jazz musicians in the world.

Nothing can keep you from fulfilling God's destiny for your life—not poverty, not discrimination, not a troubled family life. Follow the gifts God has placed in your life. Trust Him, and you will become all He has created you to be.

*Our light, momentary affliction (this slight distress of the passing hour) is ever more and more abundantly preparing and producing and achieving for us an everlasting weight of glory.*
2 CORINTHIANS 4:17 AMP

GLDB

> Faith isn't faith until
>
> it's all you're holding on to.

The story is told of a young blind man named Connie Rosemond who was playing hymns and spirituals on his guitar on Beale Street in Memphis, Tennessee, in 1919, when some men came out of a bar and asked him to play some southern blues. Figuring Rosemond was so down on his luck that he would do anything to earn some money, the men offered to pay him five dollars to play.

Standing close by, a schoolteacher named Lucie E. Campbell overheard the exchange and listened intently to see how the young man would respond. "No, I can't sing the blues for you or anybody else for five dollars or fifty dollars," Rosemond told the men. "I'm trying to be a Christian in this dark world, and I believe I've found the way out of darkness into light. I can't explain it, but there's something within me."

Rosemond's strong display of faith in God and his determination not to compromise so inspired the schoolteacher that she continued to think about the incident. Later, Campbell was moved to write the song she titled "Something Within"—a hymn that became popular among churchgoers and was the first composed and published by an African American woman. Later that year, the song was performed by Rosemond at the National Baptist Convention.

We can sense when God's presence is near. Just how sensitive we are to Him determines what our actions will be.

*Show me your ways, O LORD, teach me your paths;*
*guide me in your truth and teach me.*
PSALM 25:4-5

Gifted composer Kenneth Morris expresses his strong, personal faith in the existence of God through the writing of such popular gospel songs as *God Shall Wipe All Tears Away* (1935), *I Am Sending My Timber Up to Heaven* (1939), and *Just a Closer Walk with Thee*. But it is obvious that Morris drew from his own personal experiences when he penned the popular song *Yes, God Is Real* in 1944.

Using lyrics that go straight to the core of reality in declaring and confirming the existence of a true and living God and acknowledging that mortal man does not have all the answers, Morris became personally involved when writing: "There are some things I may not know. There are some places I can't go. But I am sure, of this one thing, my God is real, for I can feel Him deep within."

> One person with a belief is equal to a force of ninety-nine who have only interests.

A prolific and gifted composer, Morris began his career as a jazz musician in his native New York, studying at the Manhattan Conservatory of Music during the day and playing in front of enthusiastic crowds in hotels, restaurants, and lounges at night. After sickness threatened his life, Morris was forced to the sidelines for a while and later abandoned jazz to pursue gospel music.

Along with talented composer Sallie Martin, Morris opened the Martin and Morris Music Studio in 1940. The release of *Just a Closer Walk with Thee* in 1944, was followed by *Yes, God Is Real.*

Life always presents situations that cause you to wonder whether or not God is really real. When you have experienced Him for yourself, you will not have to wonder.

*Prove Me ... says the Lord of hosts.*
MALACHI 3:10 AMP

> My father gave me the greatest gift anyone could give another person; he believed in me.

Poet, songwriter, and distinguished statesman James Weldon Johnson is noted for his outstanding work in writing songs and poetry that depict the life and struggles of his African-American ancestors—those who lived during the time of slavery. But growing up in Florida with a father who was a head waiter at a resort hotel and a mother who was the first Black woman to teach in a public school system in Florida, neither Johnson nor his brother, J. Rosamond Johnson, ever experienced firsthand any of the hardship they wrote about.

James Johnson spent considerable time studying the history of his ancestors, however—learning how the slave children were taken away from their parents at an early age and sold on the auction block. He read about the conditions during that time and how every Black mother lived in constant fear that her child would be taken without warning and, like cattle sold at auction, shipped off to strange lands—never to see their families again.

In 1926, Johnson penned a song that depicted those difficult times and titled it, *Sometimes I Feel Like a Motherless Child.* The song expressed the pain and agony of a child taken away from his mother.

Like another famous song Johnson wrote, called "Lift Every Voice and Sing," this song spoke of the ongoing plight of Black people, their struggle for freedom, and the pain and suffering they endured along the path. Sadly, the lyrics depict much of what many young children, Black and white, are facing today.

A motherless feeling is an empty feeling. If this describes what you are experiencing, take joy in knowing that God has promised to be both mother and father to you—always!

*Know this: GOD, your God, is God indeed,*
*a God you can depend upon. He keeps his covenant*
*of loyal love with those who love him and*
*observe his commandments.*

DEUTERONOMY 7:9 MSG

When he was twelve, Ray Billingsley was taking a rest from a class project of decorating a twelve-foot-high Christmas tree made of aluminum cans. The youngster had begun doodling when a woman came up and asked to see his drawing.

Two days later, Ray got a telephone call from the woman, who turned out to be the editor of *KIDS Magazine*. She gave Ray a job as staff artist on her publication.

"I got five dollars for my first illustration," Billingsley remembered. "That little job kept me in Hot Wheels for a couple of summers."

Little did Billingsley know that God would use that "little" job as the springboard to usher him into a career as a successful syndicated cartoonist.

Some twenty-five years later, in 1988, Billingsley had a much more lucrative offer on the table when *Curtis*, his new daily comic strip, was launched into syndication through King Features Syndicate. One of the few comics featuring African-American characters, *Curtis*,

> Nature never made nobody. Everybody was born with some kind of talent.

whose title character is based loosely on Billingsley, currently appears in more than 250 newspapers worldwide.

Big things do sometimes come in small packages, as is evidenced by the God-given talents displayed by Billingsley—an innocent young boy from Wake Forest, North Carolina, whose only desire when he started drawing was to emulate his older brother, who studied fine arts. God took that desire and made it a reality.

Got some talent that you've been holding back? Let it go, and see how God uses it to elevate you to the next level.

*Each has his own special gift from God,*
*one of this kind and one of another.*
1 CORINTHIANS 7:7 AMP

GLDB

> Whatever is at the center of our life
> will be the source of our security,
> guidance, wisdom, and power.

Sitting behind the bench of her syndicated courtroom reality show *Judge Hatchett*, Glenda Hatchett appears to be every bit the caring, motherly type whose sole concern is not as much to mete out punishment as it is to provide guidance.

That has been Hatchett's philosophy since as far back at 1990, when she first became chief presiding judge of Georgia's Fulton County Juvenile Court. That appointment made Hatchett the first African-American chief presiding justice of a Georgia state court and head of one of the biggest juvenile court systems in the country.

"I grew up in a household with not a lot of money, but very rich in terms of caring," Hatchett once said in describing the strong influence her parents had on her while growing up in Georgia. She tells readers that her dad was a hero in their home, but it was her mother who set an example for being caring and reaching out to others. "She would recycle our clothes and take them to school because there were kids who didn't have warm coats or sweaters."

In her years on the bench, Hatchett has exhibited the influences she learned from her parents, as she strives to keep families together, promote reconciliation, and show young people that they can achieve whatever they set their minds to do.

You may not have grown up in a home filled with love and caring. Your earthly parents may not have been selfless and loving. But you have a Heavenly Father who loves you completely and selflessly. As you spend time with Him, you will learn how to pass that on to others.

*At the time, discipline isn't much fun. ...*
*Later, of course, it pays off handsomely, for it's the*
*well-trained who find themselves mature*
*in their relationship with God.*
HEBREWS 12:11 MSG

When she was a junior in college, Gwendolyn Parker's grandmother asked what kind of graduate degree she would be pursuing. The question did not come as a surprise to Parker. As the product of one of North Carolina's most successful Black families, that she would go to graduate school was a given. The only thing left unresolved was what field she would pursue.

Success was also a given. Her great-grandfather, Dr. Aaron Moore, was one of the first Black physicians in the city of Durham and one of the founders of the nation's largest Black-managed life insurance company. Her grandfather was a banker. Her father was a pharmacist who owned his own drugstore. And her mother was a math professor at a local college.

*A thing long expected takes the form of the unexpected when at last it comes.*

Parker made her mark by becoming a successful international tax lawyer and marketing manager on New York's Wall Street. But her real niche was to be found in the fulfillment of a lifelong dream of becoming a writer.

After walking away from her corporate job, Parker set out to pursue what she knew in her heart was ordained for her. In 1994, her first book, titled *These Same Long Bones*, was released. Three years later, the successful author wrote of her experiences in corporate America in a memoir she titled *Trespassing: My Sojourn in the Halls of Privilege*.

Following a career path set by others may prove profitable, but walking in line with what God has called you to do is most rewarding. There will always be those who expect certain things of you because they know you can deliver. Don't let that get in the way of what you know God has planned for you.

*The Lord is my helper; I will not be afraid.*
*What can man do to me?*
HEBREWS 13:6

GLDB

> ## Victory is sweetest when
> ## you've known defeat.

Almost from the day he entered the pro ranks, after an impressive showing as a player at the University of Kansas, professional football's Gale Sayers was a success. He scored twenty-two touchdowns in his first season with the Chicago Bears, including a record six in one game against the San Francisco 49ers—a feat that won him the NFL Rookie of the Year award.

During a seven-year career, Sayers played in 68 games in the NFL. Yet in that time, Sayers earned five All-Pro selections, set six records, and became the youngest man ever inducted into the Pro Football Hall of Fame. By the time he was forced to retire in 1971 because of bad knees, Sayers' record included leading the NFL twice in rushing and once each in scoring and kickoff returns and posting twenty 100-yard games.

He was the NFL's all-time kickoff-return leader with a career average of 30.5 yards, and he ranked third in rushing with a career per attempt average of 5.0 yards.

Only Jim Brown, at 5.22, and Mercury Morris, at 5.14, averaged more.

In addition to all his other accolades, Sayers was voted the greatest running back in the first fifty years of the NFL.

"The only thing that was void in my career was going to the Super Bowl," Sayers once said. "Everything else I did. I was All-Pro. I was in the Pro Bowl. I'm in the Hall of Fame. But I didn't make it to the Super Bowl."

For a football player, the Super Bowl is the pinnacle of success, but for a Christian, pleasing God is the chief goal. One offers rewards for this life, the other for eternity.

*We make it our goal to please him.*
2 CORINTHIANS 5:9

When entertainers like Nat King Cole, Ella Fitzgerald, and Billy Eckstine performed at the Kilby Dance Hall in High Point, North Carolina, during the 1940s, there was never any question where they would stay. Thanks to John and Nannie Kilby, African-American celebrities could always count on having a comfortable room available at the Kilby Hotel, the only place where Blacks traveling through the city could stay.

> *If you build it, they will come.*

Built between 1910 and 1913, the Kilby was no fly-by-night, rundown shack. The stately, three-story structure had all the signs of aristocracy, including arched windows with decorative hoods, spacious hallways with high ceilings, wide stairwells, and big brass beds.

The first floor of the twenty-one-room hotel housed a number of shops and businesses, where Black business owners flourished. Outside, canopies hung over the doorways of the shops.

John Kilby, a retired railroad worker, and his wife Nannie, a practical nurse and hairdresser, used their savings to build the hotel after they moved to High Point from Alamance County, North Carolina, in the 1890s.

In 1982, the Kilby Hotel was listed with the National Register of Historic Places. The year before, it was declared a historic property by the city of High Point, a fitting tribute to its builders, who used it to provide so much for so many.

In those times when you feel shunned and rejected, God provides a place for you to rest and flourish, a place where you can feel completely at home. That place is His presence. There is no better place to be in all the world.

*Jesus said, "Come to me, all of you who are weary and carry heavy burdens, and I will give you rest. Take my yoke upon you. ... You will find rest for your souls."*

MATTHEW 11:28-29 NLT

It is better to deserve honors
and not have them than to have them
and not deserve them.

Artist and sculptor Selma Burke will long be remembered in the world of art for her outstanding brass, stone, and wood sculptures. Unfortunately, when she died in 1995, at the age of seventy-five, controversy still surrounded the one achievement Burke was perhaps most proud of, but for which she never received full credit.

An interest in art came early for Burke, who used to make moldings out of clay while growing up in Mooresville, North Carolina. But to honor her parents' wishes, Burke studied to become a nurse and eventually found herself working in New York as caretaker to a wealthy infirmed heiress of the Otis Elevator family.

Continuing to pursue her interest in art, Burke was awarded a fellowship in 1935 that allowed her to study in Europe and later at Columbia University. In 1943, she won an international competition and was commissioned to sculpt a relief portrait of President

Franklin D. Roosevelt. The former president posed for Burke in 1944, and the bronze plague bearing his likeness was unveiled in 1945, five months after Roosevelt's death.

That same year, John Sinnock, the chief engraver at the U.S. Mint, was commissioned to design a new coin honoring Roosevelt. Interestingly, the image of Roosevelt on Sinnock's ten-cent piece, which was approved in 1946, looked remarkably like Burke's design. When the coin was released, it bore the initials *J.S.* on one side.

While it has been widely speculated that Burke was not officially recognized as the artist behind the image on the dime because she was African American, most records credit Burke as being the first Black sculptor to design a United States coin.

It's not unusual for others to take credit for something you do. When that happens, don't resist. God will always see that you receive credit where it counts.

*I will ... make your name famous and distinguished, and you will be a blessing [dispensing good to others].*
GENESIS 12:2 AMP

One summer when he was about ten years old, Reggie Lewis went off to summer camp and left his mother to handle his paper route. When the youngster returned from camp, he asked his mother for his earnings from the paper route.

To his surprise, Lewis' mother refused to give him the money, saying she had done all the work in his absence. After young Lewis threatened to "sue" his mother, he was finally given the money. But not before his mother imparted a piece of advice to her son that would serve him well in future business dealings: "Set your terms up front."

*People with goals succeed because they know where they're going.*

Lewis, who would come to be recognized as the "wealthiest Black man in history," never forgot those words. From his youth, he developed a strong drive and desire for excellence that was fueled by the strong work ethic of his mother and grandfather.

The inspiration and his hunger for wealth and personal success ultimately led to Lewis becoming a successful corporate lawyer and financier and owner of TLC Beatrice, a snack food, beverage, and grocery store conglomerate that at one time was the largest Black-owned and Black-managed business in the U.S. At its peak in 1996, TLC Beatrice had sales of $2.2 billion and was number 512 on *Fortune* magazine's list of the 1,000 largest companies.

When he died in January 1993 at age fifty, Lewis' net worth was estimated at around $400 million.

As was the case for this prominent businessman, some of the best advice you receive may come from those who know you best. But regardless of whom God uses to speak His wisdom into your life, be alert and listen for His input. Then put it into practice.

*[Jesus said,] "Is there anyone here who, planning to build a new house, doesn't first sit down and figure the cost so you'll know if you can complete it? If you only get the foundation laid and then run out of money, you're going to look pretty foolish."*

LUKE 14:28-29 MSG

> *Get someone else to blow your horn*
> *and the sound will carry twice as far.*

"Those who have no record of what their forebears have accomplished lose the inspiration which comes from the teaching of biography and history."

It was on the basis of these words, and a strong belief that Blacks should know something about their heritage, that Carter Godwin Woodson first established Negro History Week in 1926. His goal, according to Woodson, was to "popularize the truth. ... [We] are not interested so much in Negro History as in history influenced by the Negro."

A distinguished author, editor, publisher, and historian, Woodson believed that Blacks should know their past in order to participate intelligently in the affairs of their country. A strong knowledge of their own history, he felt, would provide for Blacks the foundation needed to become productive citizens. Recognized as the "Father of Black History," Woodson often expressed a hope for a time when Negro History Week would not be necessary because the contributions of Black Americans would be acknowledged as a legitimate and integral part of the history of this nation.

In the early 1960s, Negro History Week became Black History Week. In 1976, the weeklong celebration expanded to a month and became known as Black History Month.

You have a heritage that is celebrated every day through your personal relationship with God, your Heavenly Father. You can read about it right now. Just pick up a Bible and get started.

*God is not unjust; he will not forget your work and the love you have shown him as you have helped his people and continue to help them.*

HEBREWS 6:10

Autherine Lucy was not looking to make history when she enrolled at the University of Alabama at Tuscaloosa in April 1988. That honor had already come for Lucy some thirty-two years earlier as the first Black student to integrate the same school.

Unfortunately, Lucy was not enrolled long enough in 1956 to know what college life was like, let alone earn a degree.

The drama began on February third of that year, when Lucy attended her first class after being accepted at the university. By her third day of classes, angry mobs of students were throwing eggs at Lucy and chanting things like, "Let's kill her!" Tensions ran so high that Lucy had to be escorted to classes by police. When riots broke out, Lucy was expelled from the school by court order, for the safety of others.

For some time after her expulsion, Lucy was deemed "too controversial" and could not find work

*Someone's opinion of you does not have to become your reality.*

as a teacher though she had held credible credentials as an undergraduate.

In 1988, two professors at the University of Alabama invited the now married Autherine Lucy Foster to speak. When asked if she had ever tried to reenroll at the school, Lucy answered that she might consider doing so. Hearing her response, faculty members worked to get Lucy's expulsion lifted. In April 1988, the expulsion was overturned, and Foster was invited to reenroll at the University of Alabama. In the spring of 1992, both Lucy and her daughter graduated from the university.

Foster once considered her expulsion a failure but later came to view it as a stepping-stone to a bigger event in history—the Civil Rights Movement.

God, who is the author of time, knows just when to move on your behalf. His timing is always perfect.

*We are hard pressed on every side, but not crushed; perplexed, but not in despair; persecuted, but not abandoned; struck down, but not destroyed.*

2 CORINTHIANS 4:8-9

GLDB

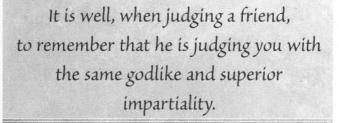

*It is well, when judging a friend,
to remember that he is judging you with
the same godlike and superior
impartiality.*

In the song "Carry Me Back to Old Virginny," American composer and minstrel James Bland wrote of returning to the place "where the cotton and the corn and tatoes grow, where the old darke'ys heart am long'd to go, where I labored so hard for old massa." Ironically, despite the song's lyrics, few people must have known the 1880s minstrel tune was composed by a Black man when it was adopted as the state song of Virginia more than half a century later.

In fact, Bland had little in common with the lyrics when he penned the popular tune. Born in Flushing, New York, his family lived far from the clutches of slavery. Bland's father, one of the first Blacks to receive a college education, was an examiner in the U.S. Patent Office—the first Black to hold that post.

Bland developed a love for music very early, singing and writing his own compositions to a banjo accompaniment. After high school, he studied liberal arts at Howard University. He applied to work with several minstrel groups, but was rejected because the groups preferred white men playing in blackface. Bland finally landed a job working with an all-Black minstrel group and was able to travel and perform.

Other minstrel tunes written by Bland include, "In the Evening by the Moonlight," "De Golden Wedding," and "Oh Dem Golden Slippers." On January 28, 1997, the Virginia senate voted to designate "Carry Me Back" as state song "emeritus" and directed a study committee to come up with a new state song.

If God judged you solely by the look on your face, would He be pleased? Thankfully, He looks at the inside to see what's in your heart where the real you resides. How are you judging those around you?

*[Jesus said,] Be honest in your judgment and do not decide at a glance (superficially and by appearances); but judge fairly and righteously.*
JOHN 7:24 AMP

Despite living under more than favorable conditions while growing up in the South during the 1940s, Johnnetta Betsch still found she had to stare the evils of segregation in the face.

Betsch could not swim at a pool located directly across the street from her house because it was for whites only. A local public library bore her great-grandfather's name. Yet, Betsch knew that the newer, better books were housed in the town's main library.

"I grew up with this duality of a family that was strong and encouraging, deeply involved in notions of faith and of community service, but in a society that challenged my worth because of the color of my skin," Betsch recalled years later about her younger days.

> *Whenever a separation is made between liberty and justice, neither, in my opinion, is safe.*

Fortunately, Betsch, who later became the first African-American woman to serve as president of Atlanta's Spelman College, had the support of her family and the encouraging words of a woman she deeply admired, Mary McLeod Bethune, who once said: "One must lift as one climbs." What Betsch saw in Bethune's words was a belief that "one has the right to lift oneself up, that aspirations are perfectly normal, to be encouraged. But to soar oneself, with no regard for others, is irresponsibility."

No matter how high the mountain of adversity in your life may be, God—who is your creator—will always see to it that you have the strength to climb over it. Where your strength may not be sufficient, He makes His available. Take advantage of it right now!

*Let us consider and give attentive, continuous care to watching over one another, studying how we may stir up (stimulate and incite) to love and helpful deeds and noble activities.*
HEBREWS 10:24 AMP

> The best preparation for tomorrow is
> to do today's work superbly well.

While most athletes look for inspiration among those in their trade, baseball great Willie Mays found his motivation in an uncle who was committed to seeing him succeed.

So determined was the uncle to see his nephew make it in baseball that he voluntarily did Mays' household chores so the youth could practice.

"My uncle would say every day, 'You're going to be a baseball player, and we're gonna see to that,'" Mays remembers. "I would have to go to school, and he would do my chores. I had to cut the wood, I had to wash the clothes, I had to do everything that everybody in the house had to do. So he would do all that stuff for me."

Eventually, the uncle's kindness would prove rewarding.

By the time he was sixteen, Mays was playing professionally with the Birmingham Black Barons of the segregated Negro Southern League. The day he graduated from high school, Mays signed with the New York Giants. And by the time he retired from baseball in 1973, Mays had garnered an impressive record that included 3,283 hits and 660 home runs.

Much of his success was due to the generous spirit of an uncle who saw potential in his young nephew and did what he could to nurture it.

God does the same with you. When He created you, He endowed you with gifts and talents. Now, He wants to bring them to the surface and help you to make the best of them. Have you recognized these abilities? And are you doing everything you can to make the most of them?

Ask God to help you, and He will.

*Let each one of us make it a practice to please (make happy) his neighbor for his good and for his true welfare, to edify him [to strengthen him and build him up spiritually].*
ROMANS 15:2 AMP

After he contracted the AIDS virus, tennis great Arthur Ashe was asked, "Is this the hardest thing you've ever had to deal with?"

Ashe's response was brief, yet deliberate: "No, the hardest thing I've ever had to deal with is being a Black man in this society."

Though he recognized his plight as a Black man struggling to succeed in a "white man's world," Ashe never allowed his struggles to become a stumbling block. Instead, he took advantage of every opportunity, following the advice of his father who once told him and his brother, Johnnie, "You gain by helping others."

> I feel that the greatest reward for doing is the opportunity to do more.

"I know I could never forgive myself if I elected to live without human purpose, without trying to help the poor and unfortunate, without recognizing that perhaps the purest joy in life comes with trying to help others," Ashe once said.

Though his life was cut short, Ashe, who died at age forty-nine, lived life to its fullest, making great strides both on and off the tennis court. In tennis, his accomplishments included becoming the first African-American male to win the U.S. championship, first to win at Wimbledon, and first to play for the U.S. Davis Cup team—highlights of the thirty-three singles titles he won as a professional.

As a humanitarian, Ashe became heavily involved as a teacher, social activist, and international ambassador. "Despite segregation, I loved the United States," he wrote in his memoir, *Days of Grace*.

In August 1988, doctors found that Ashe had been exposed to the AIDS virus while receiving a blood transfusion during a double-bypass surgery five years earlier. Even then, the strong-willed Ashe refused to let his condition hinder his commitment to helping others.

"Despair is a state of mind to which I refuse to surrender," Ashe wrote.

You can view obstacles or roadblocks in your life or as opportunities for God to work on your behalf. If you allow Him, God will either remove the roadblocks or show you how to maneuver around them.

*Whatever you do, do your work heartily, as for the Lord rather than for men, knowing that from the Lord you will receive the reward.*

COLOSSIANS 3:23-24 NASB

# As I am, so I see.

A man caught a young eagle in the forest, took it home, and put it among his chickens, ducks, and turkeys—feeding it chicken food even though it was an eagle, the king of all birds.

Five years later a naturalist was visiting. Noticing the bird, he said: "That bird is an eagle, not a chicken."

"Yes," said the owner, "but I have trained it to be a chicken. It is no longer an eagle, even though it measures fifteen feet from wingtip to wingtip."

"It has the heart of an eagle, and I will make it soar high up to the heavens," the naturalist replied.

Picking up the bird, the naturalist said: "Thou dost belong to the sky and not to this earth; stretch forth thy wings and fly." The eagle turned this way and that, then looked down at the chickens eating and jumped down to join them.

"I told you it was a chicken," the owner exclaimed.

The next day the naturalist repeated his effort.

"Thou art an eagle. Stretch forth thy wings and fly."

Again, the bird looked to the chickens feeding and joined them.

With glee, the owner again proclaimed, "I told you it was a chicken."

"Give me one more chance, and I will make it fly," the naturalist asked.

The next morning, the naturalist took the eagle outside the city, to the foot of a high mountain. The sun was just rising, gilding the top of the mountains.

Picking up the eagle, the naturalist gave his solemn instruction: "Thou art an eagle. Thou dost belong to the sky and not this earth. Stretch forth thy wings and fly."

At that, the eagle looked, but did nothing. Then, the naturalist made the bird look directly at the sun. Suddenly, the bird stretched out its wings, let out a screech, and flew away.

When you look closely at the Son of God, you will realize who you are and what you were created to do.

*God created man in His own image,*
*in the image and likeness of God He created him;*
*male and female He created them.*
GENESIS 1:27 AMP

In the book, *Narrative of the Life of Frederick Douglass,* abolitionist Frederick Douglass describes that his mistress had ceased teaching him to read at the urging of her husband and how Douglass wittingly devised a plan to trick his little white playmates into helping him learn to read:

"My mistress was, as I have said, a kind and tenderhearted woman; and in the simplicity of her soul she commenced, when I first went to live with her, to treat me as she supposed one human being ought to treat another. In entering upon the duties of a slaveholder, she did not seem to perceive that I sustained to her the relation of a mere chattel, and that for her to treat me as a human being was not only wrong, but dangerously so.

*Formal education will make you a living. Self-education will make you a fortune.*

"She was an apt woman; and a little experience soon demonstrated, to her satisfaction, that education and slavery were incompatible. ... From this time I was most narrowly watched. If I was in a separate room for any considerable length of time, I was sure to be suspected of having a book, and was at once called to give an account of myself.

"The plan which I adopted, and the one by which I was most successful, was that of making friends of all the little white boys whom I met in the street. As many of these as I could, I converted into teachers. With their kindly aid ... I finally succeeded in learning to read. ... I used also to carry bread with me ... for I was much better off in this regard than many of the poor white children in our neighborhood. This bread I used to bestow upon the hungry little urchins, who, in return, would give me that more valuable bread of knowledge."

God has many ways to get you where He wants you to go. Pray and ask Him for directions. Then, be willing to follow His instructions.

*[Jesus said,] "Be wise as serpents and harmless as doves."*
MATTHEW 10:16 NKJV

> If you don't like something change it;
>
> if you can't change it, change the
>
> way you think about it.

John R. Lewis had great hopes after the Supreme Court decision that did away with racial discrimination.

Before then, life for Blacks living in the small town of Troy, about fifty miles south of Montgomery, Alabama, was not so pleasant. White children sat downstairs in the movie theater while Blacks sat in the balcony. When he and his siblings tried to check out library books, they were told that the library was for whites only and not for "coloreds."

Desegregation meant Davis could attend a better school and not have to use hand-me-down books. No longer would he ride on a broken-down school bus or sit in overcrowded, poorly staffed classrooms.

But those freedoms were not forthcoming, and Lewis asked his parents why segregation and racial discrimination were still the norm. The only answer he got was: "That's the way it is. Don't get into trouble. Don't get in the way."

Lewis didn't get in the way. And he never got into trouble. But he did get involved. Inspired by people like Rosa Parks and Dr. Martin Luther King Jr., he joined the struggle for civil rights. He also drew from his experiences as a child, when Lewis used to pretend he was a preacher and produced a congregation that consisted of his siblings, some cousins, and the barnyard chickens.

Through the Student Nonviolent Coordinating Committee, which he helped to found, Lewis preached protest through nonviolence, leading drives to register Black voters. He also led the famous protest march in Selma, Alabama, that came to be known as "Bloody Sunday." In 1986, Lewis' efforts led to his being elected to the United States House of Representatives.

You may not understand why things are as they are, but if you can do anything to change them for the better, then do it—God's way!

*Each day is God's gift. ... Make the most of each one! Whatever turns up, grab it and do it. And heartily!*
ECCLESIASTES 9:9-10 MSG

Ron McNair was not a photographer. But in February 1984, the Black astronaut took on the title of the "world's first orbital cameraman" with the filming of *The Space Shuttle: An American Odyssey*. Sadly, the world would be watching two years later on January 28, 1986, when McNair and six other crew members were tragically killed after the U.S. space shuttle *Challenger* exploded shortly after takeoff.

Although his life was cut short at age 35, Dr. Ronald E. McNair forged a remarkable career as a research scientist and was in the forefront of laser technology with applications in the fields of satellite communications and the science of flight in outer space. A native of Lake City, South Carolina, McNair quickly achieved academic success, graduating magna cum laude from North Carolina A&T State College in 1971, and earning a doctorate in physics from the Massachusetts Institute of Technology in 1976.

In 1978, McNair was chosen from among one

> Don't aim for success if you want it; just do what you love and believe in it, and it will come naturally.

thousand applicants to be a member of NASA's space shuttle program. He completed his first space mission on the *Challenger* in 1984.

As one with humble beginnings, McNair often challenged young people to work to achieve their dreams, saying: "If I can do it, you can do it too."

On November 8, 1986, he was inducted into the South Carolina Hall of Science and Technology. In 1988, the largest planetarium in the Southeast—the Davis Planetarium in Jackson, Mississippi—named its theater the Ronald E. McNair Space Theater.

When you feel the urge to give in, remember the many times God has pulled you through in the past. He's still there today, ready to take you by the hand and walk with you. Invite Him to take charge, and then obey what He tells you to do.

*My zeal has consumed me.*
PSALM 119:139 AMP

GLDB

Having God for my friend and portion, what have I to fear? As long as it is the will of God, I rejoice that I am as I am; for man, in his best estate, is altogether vanity.

## GOD SAID

I asked God to make my handicapped child whole, and God said, Her spirit is whole, her body is only temporary.

I asked God to grant me patience, and God said, Patience is a by-product of tribulation; it isn't granted, it's earned.

I asked God to give me happiness, and God said, I give blessings; happiness is up to you.

I asked God to spare me pain, and God said, Suffering draws you apart from worldly cares and brings you closer to Me.

I asked God to make my spirit grow, and God said, You must grow on your own, but I will prune you to make you fruitful.

I asked God if He loved me, and God said, Of

course I love you. I asked My only Son to die for you so you can be in Heaven with Me one day.

I asked God to help me love others, as much as He loves me and God said, Ah, finally, you have the idea.

God may not always give you what you want, but He will always give you what you need.

*The Lord is my Strength and my [impenetrable] Shield; my heart trusts in, relies on, and confidently leans on Him, and I am helped; therefore my heart greatly rejoices, and with my song will I praise Him.*
PSALM 28:7 AMP

Funny …

- how long it takes to serve God for an hour, but how quickly a team plays sixty minutes of basketball.

- how one hundred dollars looks so big when in church, but so small when shopping at the mall.

- how long a couple of hours spent at church is, but how short they are when watching a movie.

- how we can't think of anything to say when we pray, but don't have difficulty thinking of things to talk about to a friend.

- how we get thrilled when a baseball game goes into extra innings, but we complain when a sermon is longer than the regular time.

> *Commitment means that it is possible for a man to yield the nerve center of his consent to a purpose or cause, a movement or an ideal, which may be more important to him than whether he lives or dies.*

- how hard it is to read a chapter in the Bible, but how easy it is to read one hundred pages of a best-selling novel.

- how people want to get a front seat at any game or

concert, but scramble to get a back seat at church services.

- how hard it is for people to learn a simple gospel well enough to tell others, but how simple it is for the same people to understand and repeat gossip.

- how we believe what the newspaper says, but question what the Bible says.

- how everyone wants to go to Heaven provided they do not have to believe, or think, or say, or do anything.

Funny? Not at all. How do you respond when it comes to the things of God?

*[Jesus said,] "If anyone is ashamed of me and my words in this adulterous and sinful generation, the Son of Man will be ashamed of him when he comes in his Father's glory with the holy angels."*
MARK 8:38

> When you reach for the stars, you may not quite get them, but you won't come up with a handful of mud either.

Ask most Black entertainers about their roots, and almost instinctively they will point you to the Church. It is there, they say, that the talent was born and nurtured.

It would be no different for Egbert "Bert" Williams who, in addition to becoming a famous comic, established an impressive list of "firsts" during his professional career. But while others may have derived their inspiration from what individuals *said*, Williams was inspired by some of the things those individuals *did*.

In the book, *World's Great Men of Color*, Williams recalls some of the insufferably long and boring sermons preached at his church. Instead of sleeping through the sermons, which was the habit of some, Williams used the time creatively, coming up with comedy routines based on the preacher's bald spot or a fly or mosquito that was annoying some member in the congregation. Upon returning from church, he would imitate every gesture of the preacher or the parishioner.

As an adult, Williams included the comedy in his act and soon became one of the most popular and greatest comedians of all time. Along the way, Williams established an impressive number of firsts in his career, including being the first Black to become a star comedian on Broadway (he starred in the first Black musical comedy, *In Dahomey*). He was the first Black featured in a Broadway revue and the first Black to appear in a motion picture. Williams and his partner, George "Bon Bon" Walker, became the first internationally famous team of Black stars in American entertainment.

Looking for inspiration? It's all around you. Take time, look around, and be open to the unique insights God will give you. Then use those insights to bless others.

*All Scripture is inspired by God and is useful to teach us what is true. … It is God's way of preparing us in every way, fully equipped for every good thing God wants us to do.*

2 TIMOTHY 3:16-17 NLT

When the members of some of the more formal church congregations showed disapproval at the energetic way in which a young Mahalia Jackson performed gospel music, the singer had just the right justification for her actions.

"I had been reading the Bible every day most of my life and there was a psalm that said: 'Oh, clap your hands all ye people! Shout unto the Lord with the voice of triumph!'" Jackson explained. "If I was undignified, it was what the Bible told me to do. I want my hands, my feet, my whole body to say all that is in me."

Gospel music had been a part of Jackson's life since childhood, when she went to live with her aunt after her mother's death in 1916. Secular music was not allowed in her aunt's home, so young Mahalia settled in to singing hymns and old-time gospel tunes.

During the mid-1930s, Jackson's first husband, Isaac

> *You have to give yourself entirely, then you are prepared to do anything that serves the cause.*

Hockenhull, tried to get her to ditch gospel music and switch to singing blues and popular music, so she could make lots of money. Though she tried out for and won an audition, Jackson turned down an offer from Decca Records to record blues.

Jackson also rejected the urgings of jazz musician Louis Armstrong, who told her he knew "what you can do with it" regarding singing blues. Jackson replied: "I know what I can do with it too, baby, and that's not sing it. Child, I been reborn!"

In the 1950s, Jackson's voice graced radio, television, and concert halls around the world. When she died in 1972, she was recognized as one of the world's greatest female gospel singers and the "queen of gospel music."

When you are doing what God has called you to do and your faith in Him is rock solid, it won't be possible for you to be shaken or distracted, no matter what anyone says.

*If you keep yourself pure … your life will be clean,*
*and you will be ready for the Master to use you*
*for every good work.*
2 TIMOTHY 2:21 NLT

GLDB

> Every intersection in the road of life is
> an opportunity to make a decision.

Louise Beavers had no idea she was preparing for her future in acting when she moved to California as a teenager to work as a maid for silent-screen actress Leatrice Joy. But it would be that job and the encouragement Joy provided that would lead to Beavers landing her first on-screen role.

Unfortunately for Beavers, her first job as a real-life maid for Joy would also define the parameters by which the talented actress would spend the next forty years of her acting career. But it would serve to cement her name in history as a pioneer in paving the way for African Americans to enter the movie industry.

Beavers began picking up small film roles in the early 1920s, and within three years became a full-time performer. After landing the costarring role in the 1927 remake of *Uncle Tom's Cabin*, Beavers started getting steady jobs playing maids, housekeepers, and mammies.

Her most famous role, in which Beavers broke away

from the stereotype, came in 1934 when she played entrepreneur Delilah Johnson in the movie *Imitation of Life*. The role, which saw Beavers play opposite actress Claudette Colbert, was one of the first instances in a Hollywood film where a Black woman's home life was featured on an equal basis with that of a white woman's.

On television, Beavers replaced Hattie McDaniel for one season as the maid in *Beulah*—the first TV comedy to star an African American. She also played the maid in the 1953 pilot for *Make Room for Daddy*. When she died of a heart attack in 1962 at age sixty, Beavers had appeared in more than 130 films.

The whole world really is a stage, and your audience is watching you perform. Make sure they're not just seeing you, but the God who lives inside you.

*Whatever you do, do well.*
ECCLESIASTES 9:10 NLT

When the subject of the first Black-American astronaut in space comes up, the name Guion S. Bluford should immediately come to mind. After all, Bluford was aboard the space shuttle *Challenger* in August 1983 when the spacecraft launched from Cape Canaveral in Florida.

But Bluford probably owes his seat on the *Challenger* to the fact that Robert Henry Lawrence Jr., who was actually the first African-American astronaut, never made it into space.

In June 1967, some twelve years before Bluford was accepted into the space program at NASA, Lawrence had become NASA's first Black astronaut. Several months later, on December 8, Lawrence died tragically when the F-104 Starfighter jet he was copiloting crashed at Edwards Air Force Base in California during a training flight.

Before his death, the Chicago native had

*Success is the person who year after year reaches the highest limits in his field.*

distinguished himself as an exceptional Air Force test pilot and was among the first to be named to the USAF Manned Orbiting Laboratory Program, a precursor to today's NASA space program. Bluford, who was born in west Philadelphia, joined NASA in August 1979. He flew 144 combat missions, 65 of which were over Vietnam. When he retired in 1992, Bluford had flown four shuttle flights as mission specialist and flight engineer and had logged 688 hours in space.

Whatever race you find yourself in, run to win. No doubt you will experience personal success. But who knows? You may be blazing a trail for others who come after you. If you stay connected to God, then you will always be ready to meet the challenge. Are you ready?

*In a race everyone runs, but only one person gets the prize. ... Run in such a way that you will win. ... I run straight to the goal with purpose in every step.*
1 CORINTHIANS 9:24, 26 NLT

GLDB

> I have no protection at home, nor resting place abroad. I am an outcast from the society of my childhood, and an outlaw in the land of my birth. I am a stranger with thee and all my fathers were sojourners.

An article in *National Geographic* several years ago provided a penetrating picture of what it means to dwell under the divine protection of God's wings.

After a forest fire in Yellowstone National Park, forest rangers began their trek up a mountain to assess the damage caused by the inferno. One ranger found a bird literally petrified in ashes, perched statuesquely on the ground at the base of a tree.

Somewhat sickened by the eerie sight, the ranger knocked over the bird with a stick. When he gently touched the bird, three tiny chicks scurried from underneath their dead mother's wings.

Instantly, it became obvious to the ranger what had taken place. The loving mother, keenly aware of impending disaster, had carried her offspring to the base of the tree and gathered them under her wings—instinctively knowing that the toxic smoke presented a hazard. The mother bird could have flown to safety, but refused to abandon her young.

Although the blaze had arrived and the heat had scorched her small body, the mother bird had remained steadfast—shielding her young from danger as best she could. Because she had been willing to die, those under the cover of her wings would live.

Saying you love someone is one thing, but showing your love is another. Jesus demonstrated His love by His actions when He voluntarily gave up His life so that you could live. He spread out His wings of protection and provided a covering for all believers so they could be safe. That's what true love is all about.

*[God's] huge outstretched arms protect you—*
*under them you're perfectly safe;*
*his arms fend off all harm.*
PSALM 91:4 MSG

In a single afternoon in 1935, runner Jesse Owens put on an outstanding performance at the Olympics that established him as one of the most famous athletes in the entire world. He gave four top performances, winning gold medals in the 100- and 200-meter dashes, the long jump, and on America's 4 x 100 relay team.

The medals Owens won disproved Adolph Hitler's theory that Blacks were inferior to the master Aryan race. Yet, when the popular athlete returned to the United States, he found that as a Black man he was still considered inferior.

*It is a worthier thing to deserve honor than to possess it.*

"When I came back to my native country, I couldn't ride in the front of the bus," Owens said later in an interview. "I had to go to the back door. I couldn't live where I wanted. I wasn't invited to shake hands with Hitler, but I wasn't invited to the White House to shake hands with the president, either."

While the incident bothered Owens, it did not

distract the athlete from his goal of striving to be the best in his field. Owens endured the treatment because he felt it was his job to try to make things better for his race.

James Cleveland Owens first became involved in track while in junior high school. As a teenager he set or tied national high-school records in the 100- and 220-yard dashes and the long jump. In 1936, Owens qualified for the Olympics by setting a record in the 100-yard dash.

Owens came by the nickname *Jesse* by sheer accident. At age nine, he moved with his family to Cleveland, Ohio. When a teacher asked his name, Owens answered, "J.C.," which was the name he went by. The teacher, however, misunderstood his southern drawl and thought he was saying "Jesse." The nickname stuck with Owens.

Don't wait around for the approval of others. It may never come. Be confident that God, who created you, is pleased with who you are. In the end, His is the only opinion that counts.

*[Jesus said,] "His master replied, 'Well done, good and faithful servant! You have been faithful with a few things; I will put you in charge of many things. Come and share your master's happiness!'"*

MATTHEW 25:21

GLDB

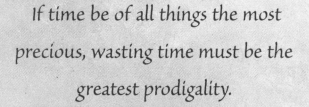

*If time be of all things the most precious, wasting time must be the greatest prodigality.*

Take time to think; it is the source of power.

Take time to read; it is the foundation of wisdom.

Take time to play; it is the secret of staying young.

Take time to be quiet; it is the moment to seek God.

Take time to be aware; it is the opportunity to help others.

Take time to love and be loved; it is God's greatest gift.

Take time to laugh; it is the music of the soul.

Take time to be friendly; it is the road to happiness.

Take time to dream; it is what the future is made of.

Take time to pray; it is the greatest power on earth.

God, who does not show favoritism, has given everyone twenty-four hours a day with which to do what needs to be done. He won't tell you how to use it, and He won't stick around to make sure you don't abuse it. That part is up to you. And so are the consequences if you waste your time.

Make the most of every second God gives you, and He will bless your efforts.

*There is a time for everything,*
*a season for every activity under heaven.*
ECCLESIASTES 3:1 NLT

While driving home after a busy day at the office, a man was passing a park near his home when he noticed there was a Little League baseball game going on. Deciding he could use a little entertainment after such a grueling day of work, he decided to pull over and check it out.

Maneuvering his car off the road and into the park's parking lot, the man got out and walked toward the ball field. Noticing the bleachers were already filled with excited spectators, he made his way over to a bench at the first-base line and sat down.

After greeting one of the young players, the man asked about the score.

"Oh, we're behind 14 to nothing right now," the youngster answered with a big smile.

"Really," the man responded, looking a bit perplexed. He wondered why the boy would appear so excited considering his team was losing.

*Courage consists in equality to the problem before us.*

"I have to say you don't look very discouraged," the man told the boy.

"Discouraged?" the boy asked with a puzzled look on his face. "Why should we be discouraged? We haven't been up to bat yet."

There is a saying that 90 percent of the things we worry about usually never happen. Faith is an act of believing you have received something before you actually see it. It gives you courage to try even harder, knowing God is with you and will never let you down.

*Be strong. Take courage. Don't be intimidated.*
*Don't give them a second thought because*
*GOD, your GOD, is striding ahead of you.*
*He's right there with you. He won't let you down;*
*he won't leave you.*
DEUTERONOMY 31:6 MSG

GLDB

> Never give up. Keep your thoughts
> and your mind always on the goal.

For twenty-two years, Leroy "Satchel" Paige had enjoyed a stellar career as the greatest pitcher in the history of the Negro leagues. His record included an impressive 64 consecutive scoreless innings, a stretch of 21 straight wins, and a 31-4 record in 1933.

But what satisfied Paige the most was the fulfillment of his dream to play in the major leagues. That happened in 1948, when at age 43, Paige signed on with the Cleveland Indians—the oldest rookie in the league.

The story goes that team owner Bill Veeck was looking for extra pitching muscle for the pennant race when he decided to give Paige a tryout. Supposedly, Veeck placed a cigarette on the ground to be used as a home plate. Paige took aim at his virtually nonexistent target and fired off five fastballs that sailed directly over the cigarette. Pleased with Paige's performance, Veeck gave him a spot on the team, and Paige went on to help the Indians win the pennant.

In 1965, Paige took the mound for the last time, throwing three shutout innings for the Kansas City Athletics. When his major league career was over, he had compiled a modest 28-31 record with a 3.29 ERA. Paige became a coach for the Atlanta Braves in 1968 and was inducted into the National Baseball Hall of Fame in 1971.

God wants you to dream big. He also wants you to let Him get involved in your dreams by bringing them to pass. What can God help you realize today? Delight yourself in Him, and He will give you the desires of your heart.

*Delight yourself also in the Lord, and He will give you the desires and secret petitions of your heart.*
PSALM 37:4 AMP

Perhaps no other fighter in the history of boxing has had more nicknames than Henry Armstrong, who at different times in his championship career was referred to by fans as "The Human Buzzsaw," "Perpetual Motion," "Homicide Hank," "Hammerin' Hank," and "Hurricane Henry." But then no other fighter in the sport's history ever held world titles in three weight classes at the same time either.

As an amateur who originally fought under the name Melody Jackson, Armstrong first won the world featherweight title in October 1937 by executing his famous "blackout punch" on opponent Petey Sarron. Less than a year later, the boxer stepped up his weight to compete in the welterweight division where he won a 15-round decision and the championship over Barney Ross.

*Victory is always possible for the person who refuses to stop fighting.*

On August 17 of that same year, the now two-time champion dropped down to the lightweight division and won a controversial 15-round decision over Lou Ambers.

Of his 174 professional fights, Armstrong recorded 145 victories and 20 losses. He had 8 draws and 1 no-decision bout. He retired in 1945 and became an ordained Baptist minister in 1951. Armstrong became one of the first inductees when the Boxing Hall of Fame opened in 1954.

When the challenge was present, size was not a factor. That was also David's experience when he went up against the giant Goliath. David knew that with God on his side, no giant would be able to defeat him. In fact, David was confident that he would slay the giant.

Victory comes in all different shapes and sizes, but you will never experience it unless you accept the challenge. There may be giants in your life, but none so big that God cannot give you victory over them.

*Thanks be to God! He gives us the victory through our Lord Jesus Christ.*
1 CORINTHIANS 15:57

> The real tragedy of life is not in being limited to one talent, but in the failure to use the one talent.

The story goes that Luther Robinson was less than pleased with his given name and suggested to his younger brother, Bill, that they switch names. When his brother refused, Luther got physical, and the exchange took place.

That, according to legend, signaled the birth of Bill "Mr. Bojangles" Robinson, one of the world's greatest tap dancers and creator of the famed "stair dance."

Born in Richmond, Virginia, on May 25, 1878, Robinson was orphaned in infancy and raised by his grandmother. When he was six, he performed song-and-dance routines in local beer gardens. As a teenager he toured with traveling companies and headlined with Cab Calloway at the famous Cotton Club in Harlem.

Robinson became famous for his popular "stair dance," which involved tapping up and down a flight of stairs both backwards and forwards. Robinson claimed to have invented the dance while being honored by the king of England. The king was standing at the top of some stairs, and Robinson danced his way up the stairs to receive the honor.

While both Black and white audiences enjoyed the unique sound of his wooden taps and his creative dance style, it was not until Robinson was fifty years old that he danced for white audiences. He had chosen to devote his early career exclusively to appearances on the Black theater circuit.

When God created you, He gave you everything you needed to live life to the full and be successful. If it was good enough for Him, it should be good enough for you. Work with what you have, and let God increase it as He sees fit.

*God has given each of us the ability to do certain things well. … Never be lazy in your work, but serve the Lord enthusiastically.*
ROMANS 12:6,11 NLT

The names *Werner Groebli* and *Hans Mauch* are not likely to mean anything to most people. But that was not the case for figure skater Debi Thomas, who became a pioneer in the sport of ice skating as the first African American to win a medal in the Olympic Games in Calgary, Alberta, Canada.

Actually, Thomas best remembered the two by their stage names of Mr. Frick and Mr. Frack, two Swiss comedic ice skaters who were famous during the mid-1930s as a star attraction with the Ice Follies. It was this duo, and Mr. Frick in particular, who served as Thomas' role model when she first started skating.

*What lies behind us and what lies before us are small matters compared to what lies within us.*

Originally, Thomas was interested in medicine as a child growing up in Poughkeepsie, New York, and actually studied biology and chemistry and attended medical school for a while on the way to fulfilling her dream of becoming an orthopedic surgeon.

By her own admission, Thomas was always one to

dream "ridiculously large dreams, and half the time they come true."

Thomas made history by winning the bronze medal at the 1988 Winter Olympic Games in Calgary—the first and only African American ever to win a medal at the Winter Olympics. Three years later, her faith in a "ridiculously large" dream moved closer to reality when Thomas graduated from Stanford and retired from skating to concentrate on becoming an orthopedic surgeon. She graduated from the Northwestern University Medical School in 1997 with plans to specialize in orthopedic surgery.

Thomas, who at one time was referred to as the "Queen of the Ice," was inducted into the U.S. Figure Skating Hall of Fame in 2000.

Learn from others, but don't try to be just like them. God created you in His image, with your own uniqueness. Dream big, work hard, and let God help you fulfill the distinct and special plans He has in mind just for you.

*You [collectively] are Christ's body*
*and [individually] you are members of it,*
*each part severally and distinct [each with his own*
*place and function].*
1 CORINTHIANS 12:27 AMP

GLDB

> *We won't even attempt to achieve what we do not believe at a deep level we can have or deserve.*

Made from a dull, off-color wood and lacking the high-gloss luster and sheen of others surrounding it, the trophy was nothing special to look at. But appearance was obviously not what was on his mind whenever NASCAR driver Wendell Scott looked at the memento he won on December 1, 1963.

Instead, the trophy symbolized perhaps the greatest moment in Scott's life—the day he became the first Black driver to win the Grand National race in the fifty-eight-year history of NASCAR.

Unfortunately, Scott would not receive the same type of accolades as those who had come before him. The South in the early 1960s was still in the grips of segregation, which accounts for the almost nonexistent celebration when Scott won the race at Jacksonville.

"Everybody in the place knew I had won the race," Scott recalled years later, "but the promoters and NASCAR officials didn't want me out there kissing any beauty queens or accepting any awards."

Undaunted, the Danville, Virginia native took it on the chin and accepted his "fame" with humility. Scott's driving career came to a screeching halt, however, in 1973 after he was banged up in a twenty-one-car pileup at Talladega Super Speedway. But his place in history as a member of the prestigious International Motor Sports Hall of Fame forever remains intact.

While some may never acknowledge the good that you do, God is not forgetful. He sees your hard work, diligence, and perseverance. And He will see that others recognize it as well.

*The Lord says, "I will guide you along the best pathway for your life. I will advise you and watch over you."*
PSALM 32:8 NLT

When fifteen-year-old Elijah McCoy couldn't get a quality education in the United States because he was Black, the youth packed his bags and headed for Scotland. After training in mechanical engineering, McCoy decided to return to the States where he could put his skills to good use.

Instead, McCoy found that nothing had changed since making his exodus. Denied employment because of his race, McCoy was forced to take a job as a railroad fireman—a move he would later be glad he took.

Around that time, locomotives needed to be shut down and lubricated periodically to prevent overheating. The frequent stops prevented railroads from being profitable. To solve the problem, McCoy invented a cup that would regulate the flow of oil onto moving parts of industrial machines. That cup, patented in July 1872 and later dubbed "The Real McCoy," revolutionized the industrial machine industry to the extent that no engines, locomotives, steamships, ocean liners, or factory machinery was

*Discovery consists of seeing what everybody has seen and thinking what nobody has thought.*

considered complete until it included a McCoy lubricator.

The phrase "the Real McCoy" soon caught on as a way of saying that people were getting the best equipment available—the genuine article and not a cheap imitation.

Be careful when it comes to plotting your course. Always consult with God when it comes to your future. Ask Him what it is you're supposed to be doing or in what direction you are to head. Even if there are a few detours along the way, His road map will never steer you off course.

*God deliberately chose things the world considers foolish in order to shame those who think they are wise.*

1 CORINTHIANS 1:27 NLT

GLDB

No race can prosper till it learns that there is as much dignity in tilling a field as in writing a poem.

A newsman probed Mother Teresa with questions regarding her zealous care for those dying in India. He seemed pleased with his acerbic interrogation, asking such things as: "Why indeed should you expend your limited resources on people for whom there is no hope?" "Why not attend to people worthy of rehabilitation?" and "What kind of success rate can your hospital boast of when most of its patients die in a matter of days or weeks?"

Staring at the man in silence, Mother Teresa absorbed the questions—trying to pierce through the facade to discern what kind of a man would ask them.

She had no answers that would make sense to him. But she did have an answer.

Speaking softly, Mother Teresa said: "The people have been treated all their lives like dogs. Their greatest disease is a sense that they are unwanted. Don't they have the right to die like angels?"

Some of the biggest tests of our faith can come through foolish questions. Knowing what to say and how to say it can go a long way toward helping others to understand you and the God you serve. When people challenge you or your faith, trust God to show you the right way to respond.

*What are mortals that you should think of us,*
*mere humans that you should care for us?*
*For you made us only a little lower than God,*
*and you crowned us with glory and honor.*
PSALM 8:4-5 NLT

As a youngster growing up in Brooklyn, New York, Lena Calhoun Horne recognized the value in the light complexion of her skin. Even the hospital staff had assumed she was Caucasian at birth.

Though not ashamed of the fact that she was African American, Horne knew her appearance could help her land better jobs that were less stereotypical as she pursued an acting career in Hollywood. When she was discovered by MGM in the 1930s, Horne stipulated in her contract that she not be cast in the stereotypical roles that Blacks in her day normally played.

The studio wanted Horne to appear darker on screen and actually had makeup manufacturer Max Factor create "Little Egyptian," a cosmetic that would help achieve that purpose. But MGM honored Horne's request, keeping her away from typical "Black" roles.

Though her first MGM role as a nightclub singer in the movie *Panama Hattie* was not credited, some

> I am not sure who I am, but I have given all of me that I can find to the pursuit of this consuming purpose, and the answer to the question is beginning to make itself known even to me.

claimed Horne's segment to be the only bright spot in the picture. Horne landed respectable roles singing in several more movies during the 1930s and making cameo appearances. She turned to singing full time in the 1950s.

Horne's active career spanned six decades, and in 1989, she was awarded a Grammy Lifetime Achievement Award. In her later years, Horne reflected on her career, saying: "My identity is very clear to me now. I am a Black woman. I'm not alone, I'm free. … I no longer have to be a credit. I don't have to be a symbol to anybody; I don't have to be a first to anybody. I don't have to be an imitation of a white woman that Hollywood sort of hoped I'd become. I'm me, and I'm like nobody else."

People will try to make you over. Recognize that God has made you just as He wanted you, and He is pleased. He created you to be a unique individual, and He has special plans that no one can fulfill quite like you.

*The Lord does not look at the things man looks at.*
*Man looks at the outward appearance,*
*but the LORD looks at the heart.*
1 SAMUEL 16:7

GLDB

> Men are equal;
>
> it is not birth but virtue that makes
>
> the difference.

For much of his life, Louisiana politician Pinckney Benton Stewart Pinchback found himself in unique circumstances because of his mixed heritage—his father was a white Mississippi planter and his mother a former slave.

On one hand, Pinchback was able to parlay his "white" ancestry to achieve some of the education, business opportunities, and material comfort normally available only to whites of that day. But there were also times when he faced discrimination.

In 1872, for instance, Pinchback was elected to the House of Representatives, but his Democratic opponent contested the election and won the seat. A year later, Pinchback was elected to the U.S. Senate but denied the seat amid charges and countercharges of fraud and election irregularities. Some observers suspected the charges were more related to the color of his skin.

Although Pinchback eventually advanced to the position of governor of Louisiana, becoming the first African American to be governor of a state, it was not by way of popular vote. He had become lieutenant governor of Louisiana in 1871, after the lieutenant governor died in office. By default, he went on to serve as acting governor of the state between December 9, 1872, and January 13, 1873, during impeachment proceedings against then-elected Governor Henry Clay Warmoth.

Once asked about his heritage and which part he drew upon as a source of pride, Pinchback responded: "I don't think the question is a legitimate one, as I have no control over the matter. A man's pride I regard as born of his associations, and mine is, perhaps, no exception to the rule."

God bestows dignity upon everyone, regardless of natural heritage. When you become His child, you can hold your head up—not in selfish pride, but looking to Him in love and faith, knowing you are deeply loved for who you are.

*I most certainly understand now that God is not one to show partiality.*

ACTS 10:34 NASB

When he was elected in 2004, Barack Obama became the only African American currently serving in the U.S. Senate. He also joined an elite group that consists of only five Blacks who have served in the Senate in the nation's history.

Hiram Revels, a barber and minister in the African Methodist Episcopal Church, made history during Reconstruction when he served as senator from Mississippi from February 1870 to March 1871. Blanche Kelso Bruce became the first Black to serve a full term in the Senate when he was elected in 1875.

> The measure of a man's success must be according to his ability. The advancement he makes from the station in which he was born gives the degree of his success.

In 1966, Republican Edward Brooke became the first African-American senator since Reconstruction; and twenty-six years later, Carol Moseley Braun of Illinois became the first Black woman ever elected to the Senate.

That he became the fifth African American to serve was a dream Obama might have expected would come true. His faith, his stride toward receiving a quality education, and his tremendous work ethic are a testament.

In his autobiography, *Dreams from My Father: A Story of Race and Inheritance*, Obama credited the success of the Civil Rights Movement for part of his accomplishments:

"As segregated as Chicago was, as strained as race relations were, the success of the civil rights movement had at least created some overlap between communities, more room to maneuver for people like me," he wrote. "I could work in the Black community as an organizer or a lawyer and still live in a high rise downtown. Or the other way around: I could work in a blue-chip law firm but live in the South Side and buy a big house, drive a nice car, make my donations to the NAACP, speak at local high schools."

When you put forth your best effort, God adds a double dose of His strength to help you out. He will open doors for you that no man can shut.

*Each one should test his own actions.*
*Then he can take pride in himself, without*
*comparing himself to somebody else, for each one*
*should carry his own load.*
GALATIANS 6:4-5

GLDB

> We may not exterminate racism, but we must believe that different racial groups can live together in peace, and we must never cease to try to build a society in which the fatherhood of God and the brotherhood of man become realities.

During the 1977 World Series between the Los Angeles Dodgers and the New York Yankees, *Sports Illustrated* reporter Melisa Ludtke was surprised when she was turned away after trying to enter the men's locker room to conduct interviews. Ludtke later learned she was being denied entry "solely on the basis of her sex."

Baseball commissioner Bowie Kuhn, it turned out, had initiated a new policy out of a concern that teams in other sports—including basketball, hockey, and soccer—were starting to allow women reporters to conduct locker-room interviews.

In a memo issued April 2, 1975, Kuhn suggested to general managers of other major league teams that baseball maintain a "unified stand" against allowing women sportswriters access to clubhouses. According to Kuhn's policy, "accredited male reporters" were allowed into locker rooms "for the purpose of interviewing ballplayers" and obtaining "fresh-off-the-field interviews." However, accredited female sports reporters were to be excluded from the locker rooms.

When Ludtke and Time, Inc., the parent company of *Sports Illustrated,* filed a federal sex discrimination suit against Kuhn, the New York Yankees, and others, the case was assigned to Federal District Court Judge Constance Baker Motley—the only female judge in the southern district of New York and the first Black woman to become a federal judge. Motley ruled that all reporters, regardless of gender, should have equal access to the athletes.

The next time someone rejects you, just remember how loving your Heavenly Father was when you gave your heart to Him. There was no rejection, only love and compassion. In fact, that is how He responds to everyone, all the time. When it comes to love and respect, there are no favorites. Everyone is on a level playing field. That's how it should be with you.

*God created people in his own image;*
*God patterned them after himself;*
*male and female he created them.*

GENESIS 1:27 NLT

In his 1980 autobiography, *This Life*, Academy-Award-winning actor Sidney Poitier recalled a time during his brief stint in the Army when he worked in a mental hospital. Poitier was so appalled at how cruelly the doctors and nurses treated the soldier patients that he feigned insanity just so he could be discharged from the military.

This first shot at acting worked for Poitier. Soon he was back in New York looking for work when he saw a newspaper ad for actors to audition at the American Negro Theater. Though he had no acting experience, and had never even seen a play, Poitier answered the ad.

> It takes a person with a mission to succeed.

The audition was a total flop as Poitier, who could barely read, stumbled through his lines in a thick Caribbean accent. He was thrown out of the audition with some advice from the director: "Why don't you get a job as a dishwasher?"

"As I walked to the bus, what humiliated me was the suggestion that all he could see in me was a dishwasher,"

Poitier recalled years later in an interview. "If I submitted to him, I would be aiding him in making that perception a prophetic one."

The humiliation was enough to make Poitier want to prove he could be more than just a dishwasher. And he did.

As one of the movie industry's pioneering Black movie stars, Poitier proved his ability in 1963 by becoming the first African American to win the Academy Award for best actor. Over the next two decades, he would go on to star in many successful films and gain widespread acceptance by audiences of all races—not because of his color, but because of his pure acting ability.

When you want something passionately, put your best effort into making it happen. Then, trust God to do the rest.

*Study this Book of the Law continually. Meditate on it day and night so you may be sure to obey all that is written in it. Only then will you succeed.*

JOSHUA 1:8 NLT

GLDB

> Perseverance is not a long race;
>
> it is many short races
>
> one after another.

From his early childhood, Michael Anderson knew he wanted a career in space travel. If a fixation on his first toy airplane, a gift from his Air Force dad, was not enough to make his desire apparent to those around him, there were other signs. Like, for example, the fact that Anderson committed to memory the names of the American astronauts. Or that he fashioned moon homes for his sister to house her Barbie dolls.

"I was always fascinated by science-fiction shows, shows like *Star Trek* and *Lost in Space*," Lt. Col. Michael Anderson would confess years later during an interview. "Going out of your house and looking up and seeing jets fly by, that seemed like another very exciting thing to do. So I knew I wanted to fly airplanes. ... I always had a natural interest in science. ... I thought being an astronaut would be the perfect job."

The forty-three-year-old African American also knew being an astronaut, and facing the unknown, was risky.

But as a strong Christian, Anderson always committed that part of his work to his faith in God.

Anderson alluded to those risks when talking with his father shortly before the space shuttle *Columbia* went into outer space in January 2003. "I know I have everything right with my Savior," Anderson said. The astronaut also told his pastor: "If this thing doesn't come out right, don't worry about me. I'm just going on higher."

When the space shuttle *Columbia* broke apart over Texas on February 1, 2003, just minutes before it was scheduled to land in Florida, Anderson and his six companions were killed. In realizing his dream, he had also gained a keen sense that God was always watching over him.

A strong, confident faith in God will cause you to go places others would never venture to go. Let Him take you by the hand and guide you there.

*[God says,] "I'll take the hand of those who don't know the way, who can't see where they're going. I'll be a personal guide to them, directing them through unknown country. I'll be right there to show them what roads to take, make sure they don't fall into the ditch. These are the things I'll be doing for them—sticking with them, not leaving them for a minute."*

ISAIAH 42:16 MSG

Pat Williams never recognized he had true leadership qualities until college when, as a young freshman, he was asked to coordinate the activities surrounding the freshman varsity basketball game. The success of that one event caused Williams to realize his God-given talent as a leader. It also opened the door for every other leadership role Williams would ever undertake in life, including that of senior vice president of the Orlando Magic basketball team.

> When someone is taught the joy of learning, it becomes a lifelong process that never stops, a process that creates a logical individual. That is the challenge and joy of teaching.

Williams' fascination with the subject of leadership also resulted in his writing *Coaching Your Kids to Be Leaders: The Key to Unlocking Their Potential*. In this Christian motivational guide, the veteran coach, motivational speaker, and father of nineteen shares his thoughts and those of some nine thousand leaders he quizzed on the subject of effective leadership among youth.

Drawing from his own experiences growing up and the encouragement he received through delegated responsibility, Williams emphasizes that young people, whether they are "natural" leaders or not, need guidance and good examples from adults in order to navigate through life and make the world a better place.

"Young people need to see their leadership role as an opportunity to serve others and God," he writes about servanthood, one of the seven elements Williams recognizes as keys to effective leadership. In his own life, he recognizes that God is his leader and follows Him closely.

"Ours is a bottom-line business, and it all comes down to winning and losing. And losing is hard," Williams says. "I have found through the ups and downs of professional sports ... that my faith, my anchor in Christ, really allows me to live up on top of my circumstances."

It is no accident that God has placed you here on Earth at this particular time. Ask Him to help you recognize and develop the leadership skills He's given you. Then use those skills to the fullest to impact your world for good.

*[The Lord says,] "Call to me and I will answer you and tell you great and unsearchable things you do not know."*
JEREMIAH 33:3

GLDB

> The practice of forgiveness is our most important contribution to the healing of the world.

It was a normal morning in September as Tom kissed his wife, Cheryl, good-bye and headed off for an early-morning flight as a commercial airline pilot. With her two teenage children off at school, Cheryl would retreat to her morning devotions and the peace she always attained through reading God's Word.

But that peace would soon be disturbed for Cheryl McGuinness with word that the plane Tom was copiloting had been hijacked and crashed into the World Trade Center in New York City. Tom, her husband of eighteen years, was gone.

Thinking back on the events of that morning—September 11, 2001—Cheryl remembers one of the last things her husband told her: "If anything ever happens to me, you have to trust God. God will get you through it. Just surround yourself with loving people, people who know Christ, people who will surround you in Christlike love."

Nearly one year later, Cheryl stood in the shadows of what had been the Twin Towers—looking into a pit at the remains of the once-mammoth buildings. The steel structure she saw resembled a cross. Fixing her eyes on it, Cheryl knew in her heart that she must forgive those responsible for her husband's death. Still, in the silence of her heart, she asked God, "Why?"

Looking back at the structure, Cheryl saw herself at the foot of the "cross." She sensed God was saying, *Because I forgave you.*

She chose to forgive.

Forgiveness is not easy, unless you first think about the forgiveness God has shown toward you. Because He forgave, you can too.

*[Jesus said,] "When you are praying, first forgive anyone you are holding a grudge against, so that your Father in heaven will forgive your sins, too."*
MARK 11:25 NLT

In March 1996, Howard Jonas made more than $100 million when his company—one of the world's largest Internet and alternative telecommunications providers—went public on the New York Stock Exchange. Four months later, Jonas' IDT Corporation released a new technology breakthrough that would eventually cut the cost of international phone calls by 95 percent.

That day, the great-granddaughter of Alexander Graham Bell, Sara Grosvenor, joined with Jonas and others in New York to use the new technology to place the first phone call ever over the network.

"Come here, Ms. Watson, I need to see you," was the message that went out when Grosvenor telephoned London to speak with Susan Cheever, the great-granddaughter of Bell's assistant, Dr. Thomas Watson.

A great moment in Jonas' life? Yes.

But it was not his best.

> *Success is sweet and sweeter if long delayed and gotten through many struggles and defeats.*

That moment had already taken place twenty-six years earlier in 1970, when a fourteen-year-old Jonas pushed his newly built hot dog stand past the old butcher shop where he had recently been fired.

"I was gloating over the fact that I was now just as independent in business as they were," Jonas later wrote in his book, *I'm Not the Boss, I Just Work Here.*

In the book, Jonas shares how he learned the importance of the Bible as God's Word and explains that as a teenager he became "religiously observant" as he began to see the patterns of biblical law in government and business. He noticed that when those principles were followed as they were intended, they ensured morality and prosperity.

God's principles work not only in the financial world, but apply to every aspect of life. He gives them freely to all who believe and will see that they work for all who apply them in faith.

*[The Lord says,] "I send [my word] out, and it always produces fruit. It will accomplish all I want it to, and it will prosper everywhere I send it."*
ISAIAH 55:11 NLT

# Tough times never last, but tough people do.

As he lay wounded during the twenty-three days of captivity in Iraq, Thomas Hamill was firm in his conviction not to show his captors any sign of fear.

Hamill had been the convoy commander on a run to deliver fuel to American troops at the Baghdad International Airport on that Friday, April 9, 2004, when the convoy was attacked. Five truck drivers and two soldiers were killed in the attack.

"I knew one thing that I'd learned since I'd been there: that you can't show fear in front of these people," Hamill said during an interview following his escape, rescue, and return to his home and family in Macon, Mississippi. "You have to show them that you've got a backbone."

His strong determination and an unwavering faith in God are what Hamill says helped him survive the ordeal.

"I prayed daily, several times a day that my Lord was

going to pick a time and a day and a place and I was going to stick with Him until He opened that door," Hamill recalled. "I said, 'I want to go home, Lord. I've got a wife and a family at home. They're going to be devastated if I die here, but I'm ready for whatever decision is made. It's Your will.'"

God opened that door on May 2, 2004, and "He let me out," Hamill now says. On that day, Hamill heard the sound of approaching troops outside the small farmhouse where he was being held. Not knowing what awaited him, Hamill rushed outside to find there was no one guarding the farmhouse. Once he saw the U.S. troops, Hamill began waiving a shirt over is head and identifying himself as an American POW!

Hamill was rescued.

Even when it seems He is nowhere around, God is always there to protect you. No matter what you face in life, He will always be there to guide you through.

*[The Lord said,] "Be strong and courageous.*
*Do not be terrified; do not be discouraged, for the*
*LORD your God will be with you wherever you go."*
JOSHUA 1:9

Bethany can still remember that moment as though it were yesterday.

It began as normal as any morning that the thirteen-year-old hit the beach in Kauai, Hawaii, to go surfing. Only this time things ended differently.

As she lay relaxing on her surfboard, waiting for the next big wave to roll in, her right hand on the board and her left arm dangling in the cool water, Bethany felt a sudden pressure and a fast tug at her arm. In an instant, a fifteen-foot tiger shark had bitten off Bethany's arm nearly to the shoulder.

During her long paddle back to shore, Bethany pushed negative thoughts out of her mind, choosing to replace them with prayer. "I'm in God's hands," she comforted herself by saying. Minutes later, as she was being whisked off to the hospital by ambulance, Bethany would find more comfort in the soft-spoken voice of a paramedic, whom she could hear praying and

> Perseverance allows you to get back on track when you hit a detour.

whispering to her: "God will never leave you nor forsake you."

Even now, over a year later, Bethany Hamilton, a devoted Christian, is still pointing to God as her source of strength and declaring her faith in Christ as she has returned to surfing. Her focus, she says, is not on the shark attack but on God, who has been with her throughout the entire ordeal. With His help, she has been able to pick up the pieces from her old life and adjust to the new one.

Regardless of any tragedy you may have faced, God is willing and able to help heal the pain from the past. Step by step He will guide you into a joyful, victorious future.

*"Fear not, for I am with you; be not dismayed, for I am your God. I will strengthen you, yes, I will help you, I will uphold you with My righteous right hand."*

ISAIAH 41:10 NKJV

> Put all excuses aside and remember this: YOU are capable.

Carla would never have envisioned herself as a candidate for the catwalk and living life as an accomplished fashion model. If her poor opinion of herself didn't keep her from ever achieving success, her natural appearance was always present to convince her that she would never amount to anything.

"I had low self-esteem," Carla remembers of her childhood. "I was thin. People called me skinny. I felt unattractive."

Low self-esteem affected Carla's daily life. She wore several layers of clothes to add bulk to her frame. And she never smiled because of a gap that existed between her teeth.

The one thing Carla Fisher did have going for her was an underlying faith in God, instilled in her as a young girl by a loving mother and grandmother who saw that she was taught the biblical fundamentals of faith. It was that influence that helped Carla realize later in life that beauty is not what appears on the outside, but within. And it was that faith that caused her not to turn and walk away one day when she was approached at a mall and asked about becoming a model.

As one of the nation's top models, Carla now sends out a message to young girls that they do not have to compare themselves to others.

"They must realize that we are all unique and beautiful," the young woman known as the "Runway Diva" says. "We are God's children—we are beautiful! If you love God and you love Jesus, then you must come to accept that 'I am who I am for a reason. I am a beautiful person.'"

God created you and is pleased with your appearance. His presence within radiates from the inside out, creating beauty that others will see too!

*Your beauty should not come from outward adornment, such as braided hair and the wearing of gold jewelry and fine clothes. Instead, it should be that of your inner self, the unfading beauty of a gentle and quiet spirit, which is of great worth in God's sight.*

1 PETER 3:3-4

Vonetta Flowers made history when she became the first African American to win a gold medal in women's bobsledding during the 2002 Winter Olympics. But though she was grateful for the honor, the achievement did not come in the area Flowers had spent much of her life training for.

Since she was nine years old, Flowers had dreamed of winning an Olympic gold medal as a track star. She had trained hard, attending the University of Alabama at Birmingham on a track-and-field scholarship and gaining recognition as one of the school's most decorated athletes. Flowers held thirty-five conference titles and victories and was the school's first seven-time All-American.

*Obstacles are those frightful things you see when you take your eyes off your goal.*

But when she failed two attempts to secure a spot on the U.S. Olympic team in 1996 and 2000, Flowers had to question whether her dream of ever winning Olympic gold was just that—a dream.

Drawing from her faith in God and the encouragement of her husband—who told her repeatedly that "God has put you in this sport for a reason"—Flowers continued to train as though she were still on the team. Little did she know it would be another team, and a totally different sporting event, that would lead her to victory and the gold medal she had so prayed for God to help her win.

In 2002, Flowers realized her dream of obtaining Olympic gold when she and her partner, Jill Bakken, made history by winning the gold medal at the inaugural Women's Olympic bobsled event. It was the first medal won by a U.S. bobsled team in forty-six years.

Have you set goals but are not sure that they line up with God's plan for you? Pray and ask Him about them. Then, trust Him to give you His direction. You can trust that He'll bring to pass His plans for you.

*Many are the plans in a man's heart,*
*but it is the LORD'S purpose that prevails.*
PROVERBS 19:21

GLDB

> The hardest arithmetic to master is
>
> that which enables
>
> us to count our blessings.

### FILL ME, LORD

- Fill me with love so that I seek to understand and appreciate the rich variety and diversity of life that surrounds me.

- Fill me with joy so that I celebrate Your presence in each and every moment I am on this earth.

- Fill me with peace so that I know how to ease those angry and sometimes violent urges that well up inside me.

- Fill me with patience so that I stop rushing long enough to witness Your miraculous work taking place all around me—and within me!

- Fill me with kindness so that I take the extra time to help the one in need, even when it isn't convenient for me.

- Fill me with faithfulness so that I place my mind,

heart, and all that I do in the service of Your Gospel.

- Fill me with gentleness so that others know that I believe in You—a God who loves and cares for all people.

- Fill me with self-control so that I act not on my impulses and urges, but rather on my beliefs and values, which are rooted in You.

- Fill me with the fruit of Your Spirit, Lord!

The Bible says in Psalm 1:3 AMP that you are "like a tree firmly planted [and tended] by the streams of water, ready to bring forth its fruit in its season." How wonderful it is to know that someone in need may pick and eat your fruit and be nourished and strengthened by it.

*You prepare a feast for me in the presence of my enemies. You welcome me as a guest, anointing my head with oil. My cup overflows with blessings.*
PSALM 23:5 NLT

The story is told of popular blues singer and guitarist B.B. King and how he came to name his famous guitar *Lucille*. It seems the singer was performing at a dance in Twist, Arkansas, one night very early in his career when a fight broke out on the dance floor. During the scuffle, a kerosene lantern fell over, and the wooden building caught fire.

At first, King fled the building and rushed to safety along with everyone else. But remembering the tool of his trade—his thirty-dollar acoustic guitar—had been left behind and determined that it would not be lost, the musician made a mad dash back into the burning building to rescue his cherished instrument. He barely escaped death during the attempt.

> *Where the determination is, the way can be found.*

When he later learned that the men had been fighting over a woman named Lucille, the artist decided to name his guitar after the woman. It would serve as a reminder never to "do a crazy thing like fight over a woman." Since that time, each of his Gibson guitars has been affectionately called *Lucille.*

King's response to the burning building and his determination to retrieve his prized possession—something most dear to him—is much like the love Jesus Christ showed when He died so that you could live. God, your Heavenly Father, would not stand by and watch you suffer or die. Instead, He sent His Son to rescue you and bring you into a new relationship with Him.

When something is really dear to you, you will do everything in your power to protect it. That's how important you are to God, who is your covering. He is always present, still ready to rescue you, no matter what problem you face.

*[Jesus said,] "If you had one hundred sheep,*
*and one of them strayed away and was lost in the*
*wilderness, wouldn't you leave the ninety-nine*
*others to go and search for the lost one*
*until you found it?"*
LUKE 15:4 NLT

GLDB

> You don't have to be great to start,
>
> but you have to start
>
> to be great.

Long before the saying *Just do it* became fashionable through the marketing strategy of sports giant Nike, basketball great Julius Erving was receiving that instruction from his mother.

"I came from a broken home, so my mom was a major influence in my life," the former NBA player recalls. "I remember hearing her say hundreds, thousands of times, 'You don't have to work that hard to try to be a good person, just do it.'"

Those words—and the constant encouragement from a strong-willed mother who understood her values—worked to instill a sense of self-worth into her children and became an anchor for Erving as he quickly realized that determination and hard work could take him a long way.

Taking his mother's advice to heart, Irving began working hard to become known as a fundamentally sound player, and this reputation followed him from high school, through college, and into the professional leagues. When he retired from the sport of basketball in 1987, Irving—then ranked number three among the top ten highest scoring players ever in the NBA with 30,026 points—was recognized as one of the greatest basketball stars of all time.

A Basketball Hall of Fame inductee, Irving is still revered as the "epitome of class" and an "ideal ambassador of the sport," because of the gracious, dignified, and disciplined manner in which he carries himself, both on and off the court.

Most of the time you instinctively know what it means to do the right thing. When it comes to a strong work ethic and being a person of character, like the commercial says, "Just do it!" God will bless you for it.

*Faith, if it does not have works (deeds and actions of obedience to back it up), by itself is destitute of power (inoperative, dead).*

JAMES 2:17 AMP

As a young boy, Charles Henry Turner found himself fascinated with the characteristics of some of God's smallest creatures and often shared his curiosities with his teachers. One day a teacher challenged the inquisitive youngster by saying, "If you want to know all those things about them, why don't you go and find out for yourself?"

Finding out is just what Turner did.

In 1907, after receiving undergraduate and graduate degrees, Turner became the first African American to earn a doctoral degree in zoology when he graduated from the University of Chicago. In the years that followed, Turner's interest would lead him to a number of discoveries about the behavioral patterns of such insects as bees, moths, ants, and cockroaches.

> For the attainment of divine knowledge we are directed to combine a dependence on God's Spirit with our own researches. Let us, then, not presume to separate what God has thus united.

Credited with being the first researcher to prove that insects can hear and distinguish pitch and that roaches can learn by trial and error, Turner also conducted research that proved bees can distinguish color patterns and discovered that light rays play a major role in helping ants to find their way.

Got questions but aren't sure where to turn for the answers? God, who is the maker and creator of the world, has the answers to every question you could ever think of. He has promised not to withhold any good thing from you and stands ready to share His wisdom and knowledge. Just ask Him.

*[Jesus said,] "Ask, and it will be given to you; seek, and you will find; knock, and it will be opened to you. For everyone who asks receives, and he who seeks finds, and to him who knocks it will be opened."*

MATTHEW 7:7-8 NASB

GLDB

> Adversity can either destroy
> or build up, depending on
> our chosen response.

With his reputation as one of the nation's most recognized motivational speakers, it might be hard to conceive that Les Brown has ever faced adversity. But that is far from the truth.

Labeled a slow learner who received no formal education beyond high school, Brown has seen his share of hardships, both as a child who was adopted when he was only six weeks old and as a successful businessman and influential author, lecturer, and television personality.

But despite those hardships, which include a divorce and being diagnosed with cancer, Brown refuses to be held back. He uses every circumstance in life to draw him closer to God and to motivate those around him to abandon any image of low self-esteem. He uses the challenges he faces to inspire others to overcome adversity and live up to their potential for success.

"I've gone through a whole lot," Brown says, "but

you'll notice that in life you will always be faced with a series of God-ordained opportunities, brilliantly disguised as problems and challenges. You just have to give thanks and just keep on moving. You can't stop."

Recognizing his "God-ordained opportunities" and putting them into action has enabled Brown to help change the lives of millions of others with a message to "live full and die empty."

He says, "Most people go to their graves with their talents, their dreams, their abilities, and their skills still in them. I say don't leave anything on the table. Become a risk taker."

Why face hardship alone when you can walk through it with God at your side and come out stronger and wiser.

*Whenever trouble comes your way,
let it be an opportunity for joy. For when your
faith is tested, your endurance has a chance to
grow. So let it grow, for when your endurance is
fully developed, you will be strong in character
and ready for anything.*

JAMES 1:2-4 NLT

311

When he was twelve years old, Herschel Walker began a daily workout program that over the next year resulted in a total of 100,000 push-ups, 100,000 sit-ups, and thousands of miles of sprints. It was a regimen that eventually prepared the youngster for a brilliant career as a high school and college football star and resulted in his winning the Heisman Trophy.

But the discipline displayed by Walker was not something he dreamed up on his own. It came from loving parents who always encouraged their children by telling them: "You are somebody ... and God loves you."

*Honor lies in honest toil.*

A strong work ethic and a sense of high self-esteem were commonplace in the household where Walker grew up. That's because Walker's parents were hard workers with strong Christian values. And they expected nothing less from their children.

"They disciplined us to do what was right," Walker recalls. "You knew what to do, and you knew what not

Additional copies of this and other titles
in the God's Little Devotional Book series are
available wherever good books are sold.

Also look for these other titles from Honor Books.
*God Has Soul:*
*Celebrating the Indomitable Spirit of African Americans*

*Soul Cry:*
*Powerful Prayers from the Spiritual Heritage of the African Americans*

*Soul Prasie:*
*Amazing Stories and Insights Behind the*
*Great African-American Hymns and Negro Spirituals*

*Voices of Hope:*
*Timeless Expressions of Faith from African Americans*

*Water from the Rock:*
*African American Edition*

❖ ❖ ❖

If you have enjoyed this book,
or if it has had an impact on your life,
we would like to hear from you.

Please contact us at:

HONOR BOOKS
Cook Communications Ministries, Dept. 201
4050 Lee Vance View
Colorado Springs, CO 80918

Or visit our Web site:
www.cookministries.com

# HONOR ⊞ BOOKS

*Inspiration and Motivation for the Seasons of Life*

to do. And whenever a child in the house went off to work, my parents made sure that he was going to *work*. … There is no such word in my family as lazy, because there is no such thing. … That's why I'm always going to give everything I've got. Because God is going to be proud of you then."

Walker applies those same principles today, explaining to young people as well as adults that a strong work ethic will cause them to become successful. "Nothing is going to come to you easy," Walker says.

God honors and blesses hard, honest labor. Whatever your hand finds to do today, do it with all your might. It will result in manifold blessings coming your way.

*All hard work brings a profit,*
*but mere talk leads only to poverty.*
PROVERBS 14:23

GLDB